Emerging Languages of Indian Sub-Continent

Prof. Bhumika Manoj Patel

Editor - **Dr. Sweta Gohel**

qurate
quratebooks.com

EMERGING LANGUAGES OF INDIAN SUB-CONTINENT
Prof. Bhumika Manoj Patel and Editor - Dr. Sweta Gohel

Published in 2025

© Published by

Qurate Books Pvt. Ltd.
Goa 403523, India
www.quratebooks.com
Tel: 1800-210-6527, Email: info@quratebooks.com

ISBN: 978-93-58983-88-3

Contents

1. Languages of South Asia 5
2. Language Family of South Asia Post Partition 10
3. Post Partition Language Trees and their Significance in India 19
4. State Official Languages of India 60
5. Languages of Union Terriotary in India 163
6. Languages of Pakistan 164
7. Official Languages of Pakistan 195
8. Major Regional Languages of Pakistan 197

Languages of South Asia

South Asia, encompassing Afghanistan, Bangladesh, Bhutan, India, Maldives, Nepal, Pakistan, and Sri Lanka, hosts several hundred languages. Prominent among these are Hindi-Urdu and Bengali, the third and sixth most spoken languages globally, respectively. The region's languages primarily include Indo-Iranic and Dravidian languages, along with Austroasiatic and Tibeto-Burman families. English serves as the international lingua franca, significantly influencing South Asian languages since the colonial era. A notable result of this influence is Hinglish, an English-influenced variant of Hindustani, widely spoken in urban areas.

Geographic Distribution of Languages:

Geo-linguistically, the Indian subcontinent predominantly features Indo-Aryan, Dravidian, and Munda language groups, collectively known as Indic languages. The region also includes language isolates like Burushaski, Kusunda, Nihali, and Vedda. The linguistic influence of the subcontinent extends to neighbouring Southern, East, and Southeast Asian regions, forming an extended linguistic area known as the Indo sphere. The sprachbund of Indic and neighbouring languages is referred to as South Asian languages, which also encompass Eastern-Iranic, Nuristani, Central, and Western Tibeto-Burman languages.

The Iranian Plateau to the west of the subcontinent hosts Iranic languages, including Pashto in Pashtunistan and Balochi in Balochistan. Kafiri languages are spoken in northern pockets of the plateau and the subcontinent. The Trans-Himalayan Tibeto-Burman languages and Khasi–Palaungic languages of the Austroasiatic family are found in the Himalayan and Indo-Burman Ranges, mainly on the Tibetan Plateau and in Burma. Andamanese languages are spoken on the Andaman Islands.

Distribution by Country:

Afghanistan:

- **Official Languages**: Pashto and Dari (Farsi), both Iranic languages.

Dari:

- Afghan standardized register of Persian.
- Considered the lingua franca of Afghanistan.
- Used in Afghan literature.

Tajik:

- Spoken by people near Tajikistan.
- Officially regarded as the same as Dari.

Pashto:

- Widely spoken by Pashtun people.
- Mainly reside in the south, near the Pakistani-Afghan border.

Turkic Languages:

- Uzbek and Turkmen spoken near Uzbekistan and Turkmenistan.

Bangladesh:

- **National Language**: Standard Bengali (based on the Rarhi dialect).
- **Majority Language**: Eastern Bengali.
- **Native Languages**: Sylheti and Chittagonian.
- **Ethnic Minority Languages**: Tibeto-Burman, Dravidian, and Austro-Asiatic languages.

Bhutan:

- **National Language**: Dzongkha.
- **Other Languages Spoken**: Brokpa, Dzala, Chali, Chocangacakha, Dakpa, Khengkha, Nepali, Gongduk, Nyenkha, Lhokpu, Takpa, Tshangla.
- **Language Families**: Mostly Tibetic languages. /Nepali (Indo-Aryan language).

India:

- **Language Families**:
- Indo-Aryan, Dravidian, Austroasiatic (Munda), Tibeto-Burman.
- Some Himalayan languages remain unclassified.
- 461 living languages listed by SIL Ethnologue.
- **Most Widespread Language**:
- Hindustani.
- "Hindi" includes a broad variety of Hindi languages, with native speakers accounting for 39% of the population.
- **Second Most Spoken Language**:
- Bengali, found in Bangladesh and Indian states of West Bengal, Tripura, and Assam.
- **International Mother Language Day**:
- Created by UNESCO to commemorate the Bengali language.
- **Notable Languages**:

- Odia, Telugu, Punjabi, Marathi, Tamil, Urdu, Sindhi, Kannada, Pashto, Malayalam, Maithili, Meitei (Manipuri), Konkani, Tulu.
- Thirteen languages account for over 95% of the population; all are "scheduled languages of the Constitution."
- **Scheduled Languages Spoken by Less Than 1%**:
- Santali, Meitei (Manipuri), Bodo, Dogri.
- **Largest Non-Scheduled Languages**:
- Bhili, followed by Gondi, Tulu, and Kurukh.

Maldives:

- **National Language**: Divehi, spoken by 95% of the population.
- **Religious Language**: Arabic.
- **Language of Instruction and International Use**: English.

Nepal:

- **Language Families**: Indo-Aryan and Sino-Tibetan.
- **Official Language**: Nepali (formerly Gorkhali), spoken by the majority.
- **Indo-Aryan Languages in Nepal**: Maithili, Bhojpuri, Tharu (southern Nepal in the Terai region).
- **Sino-Tibetan Languages in Nepal**: Tamang, Newari, Magar, Gurung, Kiranti, Sherpa (central and northern regions).

Pakistan:

- **Major Language Families**: Indo-Iranian (western regions: Iranic languages; eastern regions: Indo-Aryan languages).
- **Other Language Families**: Dravidian (Brahui in Central Balochistan), Sino-Tibetan (Balti, Purgi in the north-east), Nuristani (Kamkata-vari in the north-west), Language Isolate (Burushaski in the north), Turkic (Kyrgyz, Uzbeks, Turkmen).
- **National Language**: Urdu, a Persian zed register of Hindustani.

- **Major Native Languages**: Punjabi, Saraiki, Sindhi, Baluchi, Pashto.
- **Other Languages**: Over 70 languages including Shina, Balti, Gujarati, Bengali.

Sri Lanka:

- **Official Languages**: Sinhala and Tamil.
- **Link Language**: English.
- **Language Families**: Tamil (South-Dravidian), Sinhala (Insular Indic, related to Dhivehi of Maldives).
- **Indigenous Language**: Vedda, predating Indo-Aryan and Dravidian arrivals.

Language Family of South Asia Post Partition

Ethnolinguistically, South Asia's languages reflect the region's complex history and geography, forming a diverse patchwork of language families, phyla, and isolates. In India, languages belong to several families, with the major ones being Indo-Aryan, spoken by 78.05% of the population, and Dravidian, spoken by 19.64%. These two families are the most significant in terms of the number of speakers, highlighting the linguistic richness and diversity of the Indian subcontinent.

1. Indo-European Language Family in India:

- **Largest Language Family**:
- Indo-Aryan, a branch of the Indo-Iranian family.
- Indo-Iranian is the easternmost subfamily of the Indo-European language family.
- **Prevalence**:
- Indo-Aryan languages account for about 1,035 million speakers, over 76.5% of India's population (2018 estimate).

- **Most Widely Spoken Indo-Aryan Languages**:
- Hindi, Bengali, Marathi, Urdu, Gujarati, Punjabi, Kashmiri, Marwari, Sindhi, Assamese (Asamiya), Maithili, Odia.
- **Other Indo-European Languages**:
- English is prominent as a lingua franca.

2. Dravidian Language Family:

- **Size and Distribution**:
- Second largest language family in India.
- Accounts for approximately 277 million speakers (20.5% of the population, 2018 estimate).
- Spoken mainly in southern India, parts of eastern and central India, and northeastern Sri Lanka.
- Also found in parts of Pakistan, Nepal, and Bangladesh.
- **Major Dravidian Languages**: Telugu, Tamil, Kannada, Malayalam.
- **Speakers Beyond Mainstream Population**:
- Also spoken by small scheduled tribes like the Oraon and Gond.
- **Languages Exclusively Spoken Outside India**:
- Brahui in Balochistan, Pakistan.
- Dhangar (a dialect of Kurukh) in Nepal.

3. Austroasiatic Language Family:

- **Prevalence**: Smaller language family with about 10 million speakers (approximately 3% of the population).
- **Geographic Distribution**: Native to Southeast Asia, with migration to India.
- **Austroasiatic Languages in India**:
- **Mainland India**: Khasi and Munda languages, including Bhumij and Santali.
- **Nicobar Islands**: Also part of the Austroasiatic family.
- **Status**: Except for Khasi and Santali, most Austroasiatic languages in India are endangered.

4. Sino-Tibetan Language Family:

- **Size and Scope**:
- Comprises more than 400 languages.
- Second largest language family by number of native speakers, with around 1.4 billion speakers.
- **Major Languages**:
- **Sinitic Languages**: Predominant, with approximately 1.3 billion speakers.
- **Burmese**: About 33 million speakers.
- **Tibetic Languages**: Around 6 million speakers.
- **Geographic Distribution**:
- Spoken across the Himalayas, Southeast Asian Massif, and the eastern edge of the Tibetan Plateau.
- Many languages are spoken in remote mountain areas with small, poorly documented speech communities.
- **Linguistic Research**:
- Several subgroups have been reconstructed, but a comprehensive proto-language for the entire family is still under research.
- Traditionally divided into Sinitic (Chinese languages) and Tibeto-Burman branches, though a common origin for non-Sinitic languages has not been established.
- **Controversial Inclusions**:
- Kra–Dai and Hmong–Mien languages are included by some Chinese linguists but are generally excluded by the international community.
- Various links to other language families have been proposed but lack broad acceptance.

5. Tibeto-Burman Language Family:

- **Representation in India**:
- Well-represented across the Indian subcontinent.

- Relationships among languages are complex and not easily discernible, described as a "patch of leaves on the forest floor" rather than a "family tree."
- **Notable Scholar**: Suniti Kumar Chatterjee, a Padma Vibhushan awardee, highlighted Meitei (Manipuri) as particularly significant in literature compared to other Tibeto-Burman languages like Newari.
- **Geographic Distribution in India**:
- Spoken across the Himalayas and north eastern regions, including: Arunachal Pradesh, Assam (hills and autonomous councils), Himachal Pradesh, Ladakh, Manipur, Meghalaya, Mizoram, Nagaland, Sikkim, Tripura, West Bengal
- **Sino-Tibetan Languages in India**:
- **Constitutionally Recognized Official Languages**: Meitei (Manipuri), Bodo
- **Non-Scheduled Languages**: Karbi, Lepcha and Various Tibetic, West Himalayish, Tani, Brahmaputran, Angami–Pochuri, Tangkhul, Zeme, Kukish sub-linguistic branches, among others.

6. Tai-Kadai Language Family:

- **Historical Context**:
- The Ahom language, a South western Tai language, was once dominant in the Ahom Kingdom in modern-day Assam but has since been replaced by Assamese.
- **Current Distribution**:
- Small Tai communities and languages are present in Assam and Arunachal Pradesh.
- Notable Tai languages in these regions include Tai Phake, Tai Aiton, and Tai Khamti.
- **Linguistic Similarities**:
- These Tai languages are similar to: Shan (Shan State, Myanmar), Dai (Yunnan, China), Lao (Laos), Thai (Thailand), Zhuang (Guangxi, China)

7. Great Andamanese Language Family:

- **Great Andamanese Languages**:
- **Languages**:
    - **Extinct Languages**: Several extinct languages within this group.
    - **Endangered Language**: Aka-Jeru (highly endangered).
- **Ongan Language Family**:
- **Languages**:
    - **Extant Languages**: Önge and Jarawa.
    - **Extinct Language**: Jangil.
- **Sentinelese**: Likely related to the Great Andamanese and Ongan languages.

8. Language Isolates in South Asia:

- **Indian Mainland**:
- **Nihali**: Considered a language isolate with ambiguous status. It has been classified as a distinct Austroasiatic language, a dialect of Korku, or even a "thieves' argot."
- **South Asia (Other Regions)**:
- **Burushaski**: Spoken in Gilgit–Baltistan (administered by Pakistan).
- **Kusunda**: Found in western Nepal.
- **Vedda**: Spoken in Sri Lanka.
- **Great Andamanese**: The status as a language family is debated, with some considering it a language isolate.
- **Bantu Language**:
- **Sidi**: A Bantu language spoken in Gujarat by the Siddi until the mid-20th century.

Language Family of India:

Overview of Languages in India:

- **Major Language Families**:
- **Indo-Aryan Languages**: Spoken by 78.05% of Indians.

- **Dravidian Languages**: Spoken by 19.64% of Indians.
- **Together Known as**: Indic languages.
- **Minor Language Families and Isolates**:
- Spoken by the remaining 2.31% of the population.
- Includes Austroasiatic, Sino-Tibetan, Tai-Kadai, and other minor families and isolates.
- **Number of Languages**:
- **People's Linguistic Survey of India**: Lists 780 languages.
- **Ethnologue**: Lists 456 languages.
- **Official Languages**:
- **Article 343**: Hindi (Devanagari script) is the official language, with English continuing for 15 years from 1947.
- **Official Languages Act, 1963**: Allows for the indefinite use of English alongside Hindi.
- **Numerals**: International form of Indian numerals (Arabic numerals) used for official purposes.
- **Constitutional Status**:
- No national language is designated by the Constitution of India.
- **Eighth Schedule**: Lists 22 scheduled languages with recognition, status, and official encouragement.
- **Classical Languages**: Kannada, Malayalam, Odia, Sanskrit, Tamil, and Telugu.
- **Census and Language Statistics**:
- **2001 Census**: 122 major languages and 1599 other languages.
- **Languages with More Than a Million Speakers**: 30 languages.
- **Languages with More Than 10,000 Speakers**: 122 languages.
- **Historical Contact Languages**:
- **Persian**: Used during the Mughal period as a court and administrative language.

- **English**: Continues to be important in higher education and government.
- **Current Linguistic Dynamics**:
- **Hindi**: Largest number of first-language speakers, serves as a lingua franca in northern and central India. Concerns about its imposition in non-Hindi regions like Tamil Nadu, Karnataka, Maharashtra, West Bengal, Assam, and Punjab.
- **Bengali**: Second most spoken language, prominent in eastern and north eastern regions.
- **Marathi**: Third most spoken, significant in south western India.
- **Telugu**: Commonly spoken in south eastern regions.
- **Language Growth**:
- **Fastest Growing Languages**: Hindi, followed by Kashmiri, Meitei (Manipuri), Gujarati, and Bengali according to the 2011 Census.
- **Ethnologue Language Breakdown**:
- **Sino-Tibetan**: 148 languages.
- **Indo-European**: 140 languages.
- **Dravidian**: 84 languages.
- **Austro-Asiatic**: 32 languages.
- **Andamanese**: 14 languages.
- **Kra-Dai**: 5 languages.

Classical Languages of India:

- **Definition**:
- Indian classical languages, or Shastriya Bhasha, refer to languages with high antiquity and valuable, original, and distinct literary heritage.
- **Recognition**:
- **Official Recognition**: In 2004, the Government of India established criteria for granting the status of "Classical Language" to languages with significant literary and historical value.

- **Linguistic Experts' Committee**: Formed by the Ministry of Culture to evaluate and recommend languages for classical status.
- **Officially Recognized Classical Languages**: Kannada, Malayalam, Odia, Sanskrit, Tamil, Telugu
- **Local Names**:
    - Sashtriya Bhasha (Odia)
    - Shreshtha Bhasha (Malayalam)
    - Chemmoli (Tamil)
- **Unrecognized Classical Languages**:
- **Description**: Languages considered classical by scholars but not officially recognized by the Government of India.
- **Status**: These languages may have official or scheduled language status but lack formal "classical" designation.

Classical Languages and Literature:

- **Pali**:
- **Description**: A classical language liturgical to Theravada Buddhism.
- **Origin**: Northern India; closely related to Old Indo-Aryan and Vedic Sanskrit, but not a direct descendant.
- **Historical Usage**: Pali became widely used because Buddha opposed Sanskrit for Buddhist writings.
- **Historical Evidence**: Written records date back to the 1st century BCE, with oral transmission from around the 3rd century BCE.
- **Meitei**:
- **Description**: Also known as Manipuri, a classical language of the Sino-Tibetan family.
- **Literary Tradition**: Has a literary tradition of over 2000 years.
- **Notable Works**:
    - Ougri: Musical composition from around the 1st century CE.

    - Poireiton Khunthok: Narrative text from around the 3rd century CE.
    - Khencho: Musical composition before the 7th century CE.
    - Copper Plate Inscriptions: 6th-7th century CE inscriptions of King Khongtekcha.
    - Panthoibi Khonggul: Narrative text from around the 8th century CE.
    - Loiyumpa Silyen: Written Constitution from the 11th-12th century CE.
- **Cultural Significance**: Known for its classical association with Manipuri classical dance and the Meitei civilization's rich cultural heritage.
- **Classical Epic**: Khamba Thoibi Sheireng (Epic of Khamba Thoibi) is the third-longest Indian epic poem with 39,000 lines and regarded as the national epic of the Manipuris.
- **Recognition Movement**: Efforts since 2013 to gain official classical language status, supported by the Government of Manipur, civil society organizations, and language experts.

Post Partition Language Trees and their Significance in India

1. Indo Aryan Language Family:

The Indo-Aryan languages, a sub-branch of the Indo-European family, are spoken primarily in India, Pakistan, Bangladesh, Nepal, Sri Lanka, and the Maldives, with at least 640 million speakers according to the 1981 census. These languages, which include Hindi, Bengali, and Punjabi among others, form part of the Indo-Iranian subgroup, alongside Iranian languages such as Persian and Pashto. The Indian subcontinent serves as a dialect continuum where linguistic variations transition smoothly across regions due to minimal geographical barriers, facilitating the movement and interaction of speakers.

The Hindi Belt: The Hindi Belt encompasses a large region in Northern India where Hindi is the official language. According to the Ethnologue (1999), 491 million people speak Hindi as their first language, while 58 million speak Urdu as their first language. Despite Hindi's official status, the region is linguistically diverse, with several distinct languages. Grierson's classification (1883, 1969) divides the Hindi dialect area into subgroups:

- **Western Hindi**: Includes Braj, Kannauji, and Haryanvi.
- **Eastern Hindi**: Comprises Awadhi, Bagheli, and Chhattisgarhi.
- **Bihari**: Encompasses Bhojpuri, Magahi, and Maithili.
- **Central Pahari**: Includes Kumauni and Garhwali.
- **Rajasthani**: Contains Marwari, Mewari, Harauti, and Malvi.

Languages East of the Hindi Belt:

- **Assamese**: Spoken in Assam.
- **Bengali**: Spoken in West Bengal, Tripura, and Bangladesh.
- **Oriya**: Spoken in Odisha.
- **Bishnupriya Manipuri**: Closely related to Bihari languages like Bhojpuri, Magahi, and Maithili.

Central Indo-Aryan:

- **Eastern Punjabi**
- **Rajasthani**: Includes Marwari, Mewari, Harauti, Malvi.
- **Bhil Languages**: Bhili, Garasia, Rathawi, Wagdi; located near Rajasthani, Gujarati, and Marathi.
- **Gujarati**: Includes Saurashtra.
- **Modern Standard Hindi**: Falls under Central Indo-Aryan.
- **Romani and Parya**: Central Indo-Aryan languages spoken outside the subcontinent in Tajikistan and Uzbekistan.

Northern and North-Western Indo-Aryan:

Pahari (Hill) Languages:

- **Eastern**: Nepali (spoken in Nepal, West Bengal, Sikkim, Bhutan)
- **Central**: Garhwali, Kumauni.
- **Western**: Dogri/Kangri, Jaunsari, Bilaspuri.

North-Western Indo-Aryan:

- **Dardic**: Includes languages such as Khowar, Kalasha.
- **Sindhi**: Spoken in Sindh (Pakistan) and Kachchhi (Gujarat).

- **Lahnda**: Includes Hindko, Western Punjabi, Saraiki/Siraiki.
- **Kashmiri**: Spoken in Kashmir.
- **Kohistani**: Includes Tirahi, Torwali.
- **Kunar**: Includes Gawar-Bati, Shumashti.
- **Shina**: Includes Brokskat/Brokpa, Domaki, Savi, Shina.

Note: Dardic languages were previously grouped with Nuristani languages, but since Strand (1973), Nuristani languages (e.g., Ashkun, Kati/Bashgali, Prasuni, Tregami, Waigali) are now analyzed as sister languages to both Indo-Aryan and Iranian language families.

The Non-Indo-Aryan Neighbourhood:

- **Dravidian Language Family**:
  - **Languages**: Tamil, Kannada, Telugu, Malayalam.
  - **Historical Contact**: Dravidian languages may have been spoken in parts of North India before Indo-Aryan languages became dominant.
  - **Influence**: Clear influence on Indo-Aryan languages in regions near Dravidian-speaking areas, such as Marathi and Oriya, and possibly Gujarati.
- **Iranian Language Family**:
  - **Languages**: Pashto, Dari, Persian, Baluchi, Ormuri.
- **Language Isolate**:
  - **Burushaski**: Spoken in Gilgit-Baltistan (Pakistan).
- **Austroasiatic Language Family**:
  - **Mon-Khmer**: Includes Amwi, Khasi, Pnar/Jaintia.
  - **Munda**: Includes Mundari, Juang, Khariya, Gorum, Ho.
- **Tibeto-Burman Language Family**:
  - **Languages**: Kiranti, Newari, Meithei, Lepcha, Tangkhul, Hmar.

2. Dravidian Language Family:

- **Geographic Distribution**: Spoken by approximately 250 million people primarily in southern India, north-eastern Sri Lanka, and south-western Pakistan. There are also diaspora communities in Southeast Asia, the Middle East,

Europe, North America, and Oceania.

- **Historical Evidence**: First attested in the 2nd century BCE with inscriptions in Tamil-Brahmi script found in Tamil Nadu.
- **Major Languages**:
  - **Telugu**: Largest in terms of speakers.
  - **Tamil**: Has a long literary tradition and historical significance.
  - **Kannada**: Prominent in Karnataka with a rich literary history.
  - **Malayalam**: Spoken in Kerala, with a well-developed literary tradition.
- **Smaller Languages**:
  - **Tulu** and **Kodava**: Smaller literary languages.
  - **Gondi**: Spoken in central India.
  - **Malto** and **Kurukh**: Spoken in isolated areas of eastern India; Kurukh also extends to Nepal, Bhutan, and Bangladesh.
  - **Brahui**: Spoken in Balochistan (Pakistan), Iran, Afghanistan, and Turkmenistan.
- **Cultural and Historical Influence**: Dravidian languages influenced place names and grammatical features in Indo-Aryan languages such as Marathi, Gujarati, Marwari, and Sindhi, suggesting a historical spread across the Indian subcontinent.
- **Origins and Relationships**: Although there is speculation about migrations from the Iranian plateau, proto-Dravidian vocabulary suggests an indigenous origin in India. Despite extensive research, no definitive relationship with other language families has been established.

North Dravidian Languages:

- **Brahui**: Spoken in Balochistan (Pakistan), parts of Helmand (Afghanistan), Beluchistan, and Kerman (Iran).

- **Kurukh**: Found in Chhattisgarh, Jharkhand, Odisha, West Bengal, and Bihar (India), as well as parts of Nepal, Bhutan, and Bangladesh.
- **Malto**: Spoken in Bihar, Jharkhand, and West Bengal (India).
- **Kurambhag Paharia**: Found in Jharkhand, West Bengal, and Odisha.

Central Dravidian Languages:

- **Kolami**: Spoken in Maharashtra and Telangana.
- **Duruwa**: Found in Odisha, Chhattisgarh, and Andhra Pradesh.
- **Ollari**: Spoken in Odisha and Andhra Pradesh.
- **Naiki**: Found in Maharashtra.

South Dravidian Languages:

- **Tamil**: Predominantly spoken in Tamil Nadu, Puducherry, and parts of Andhra Pradesh, Karnataka, Kerala, Telangana, Maharashtra, Gujarat, Delhi, and several international locations including Sri Lanka, Singapore, and Malaysia.
- **Kannada**: Mainly spoken in Karnataka, parts of Kerala, Maharashtra, Tamil Nadu, Andhra Pradesh, Telangana, and also in international locations such as the United States, Australia, and Germany.
- **Malayalam**: Spoken in Kerala, Lakshadweep, Mahe district (Puducherry), parts of Karnataka, Tamil Nadu, Maharashtra, and several international regions including the UAE, the US, and the UK.
- **Tulu**: Found in Karnataka (Dakshina Kannada, Udupi) and Kerala (Kasaragod), with significant diaspora in cities like Mumbai and Thane and Gulf countries.
- **Beary**: Spoken in Karnataka (Dakshina Kannada, Udupi) and Kerala (Kasaragod), with diaspora in Gulf countries.
- **Pattapu**: Found in Andhra Pradesh.
- **Irula**: Spoken in Tamil Nadu (Nilgiris district) and Karnataka (Mysore district).

- **Kurumba**: Found in Tamil Nadu (Nilgiris district).
- **Badaga**: Spoken in Karnataka (Mysore district) and Tamil Nadu (Nilgiris district).
- **Kodava**: Found in Karnataka (Kodagu district).
- **Jeseri**: Spoken in Lakshadweep.
- **Yerukala**: Found in Karnataka, Kerala, Andhra Pradesh, Tamil Nadu, and Telangana.
- **Betta Kurumba**: Spoken in Karnataka (Chamarajanagar, Kodagu, Mysore districts), Kerala (Wayanad), and Tamil Nadu (Nilgiris).
- **Kurichiya**: Found in Kerala (Kannur, Kozhikode, Wayanad).
- **Ravula**: Spoken in Karnataka (Kodagu) and Kerala (Kannur, Wayanad).
- **Mullu Kurumba**: Found in Kerala (Wayanad) and Tamil Nadu (Nilgiris).
- **Sholaga**: Spoken in Tamil Nadu and Karnataka (Mysore district).
- **Kaikadi**: Found in Madhya Pradesh (Betul) and Maharashtra (Amravati).
- **Paniya**: Spoken in Karnataka (Kodagu), Kerala, and Tamil Nadu.
- **Kanikkaran**: Found in Kerala and Tamil Nadu (Kanyakumari, Tirunelveli).
- **Malankuravan**: Spoken in Tamil Nadu (Kanyakumari) and Kerala (Kollam, Kottayam, Thiruvananthapuram).
- **Muthuvan**: Found in Andhra Pradesh, Kerala, and Tamil Nadu (Coimbatore, Madurai).
- **Koraga**: Spoken in Karnataka (Dakshina Kannada, Udupi) and Kerala (Kasaragod).
- **Kumbaran**: Found in Kerala (Kozhikode, Malappuram, Wayanad).
- **Paliyan**: Spoken in Kerala (Idukki, Ernakulam, Kottayam), Tamil Nadu, and Karnataka.

- **Malasar**: Found in Kerala (Palakkad) and Tamil Nadu (Coimbatore).
- **Malapandaram**: Spoken in Kerala (Kollam, Pathanamthitta) and Tamil Nadu (Coimbatore, Madurai, Viluppuram).
- **Eravallan**: Found in Kerala (Palakkad) and Tamil Nadu (Coimbatore).
- **Wayanad Chetti**: Spoken in Karnataka, Kerala (Wayanad), and Tamil Nadu (Coimbatore, Nilgiris, Erode).
- **Muduga**: Found in Kerala (Palakkad) and Tamil Nadu (Coimbatore, Nilgiris).
- **Thachandan**: Spoken in Kerala (Malappuram, Wayanad).
- **Kadar**: Found in Kerala (Thrissur, Palakkad) and Tamil Nadu (Coimbatore).
- **Toda**: Spoken in Karnataka (Mysore) and Tamil Nadu (Nilgiris).
- **Attapady Kurumba**: Found in Kerala (Palakkad).
- **Kunduvadi**: Spoken in Kerala (Kozhikode, Wayanad).
- **Mala Malasar**: Found in Kerala (Palakkad) and Tamil Nadu (Coimbatore).
- **Pathiya**: Spoken in Kerala (Wayanad).
- **Kota**: Found in Tamil Nadu (Nilgiri district).
- **Kalanadi**: Spoken in Kerala (Wayanad).
- **Holiya**: Found in Madhya Pradesh (Balaghat, Seoni), Maharashtra and Karnataka.
- **Allar**: Spoken in Kerala (Palakkad, Malappuram).
- **Aranadan**: Found in Kerala (Malappuram).
- **Vishavan**: Spoken in Kerala (Ernakulam, Kottayam, Thrissur).

Unclassified and Extinct Dravidian Languages:

Unclassified Dravidian Languages:

- **Khirwar**: Spoken in the Surguja district of Chhattisgarh.

- **Kumbaran**: Found in Kerala (also listed under South Dravidian languages).
- **Cholanaikkan**: Located in the Malappuram district of Kerala.
- **Kakkala**: Spoken in Kerala.

Extinct Dravidian Languages:

- **Malaryan**: Once spoken in Kerala and Tamil Nadu; classified under the Malayalamoid branch.
- **Nagarchal**: Previously found in Madhya Pradesh (Balaghat, Chhindwara, Jabalpur, Mandla, and Seoni districts); part of the Gondic branch.
- **Ullatan**: Previously spoken in Kerala; classified under the Malayalamoid branch.

Austroasiatic Language Family:

- **Geographic Distribution**: Spoken across mainland Southeast Asia, South Asia, and parts of East Asia, including countries like Vietnam, Cambodia, Thailand, Laos, India, Myanmar, Malaysia, Bangladesh, Nepal, and southern China.
- **Speakers**: Around 117 million people speak Austroasiatic languages, with Vietnamese as the most widely spoken, followed by Khmer and Mon.
- **National Languages**:
  - **Vietnamese** in Vietnam
  - **Khmer** in Cambodia
  - **Mon** in Myanmar and Thailand
  - **Wa** as a national language in Myanmar's Wa State
  - **Santali** is one of India's 22 scheduled languages.
- **Language Classification**:
  - Ethnologue lists 168 Austroasiatic languages.
  - Traditionally divided into **Mon–Khmer** and **Munda** groups.

- Recent classifications suggest three groups: **Munda**, **Mon-Khmer**, and **Khasi–Khmuic**, or merge Mon–Khmer with the broader family.
- **Origins**: Austroasiatic languages are indigenous to mainland Southeast Asia, preceding Kra–Dai, Hmong-Mien, Austronesian, and Sino-Tibetan languages.
- **Etymology**: The term "Austroasiatic" combines the Latin "auster" (meaning "south") with "Asia."
- **Regional Branches**: Only Khasic, Munda, and Nicobarese branches are found in South Asia.
- **Classification Debate**: The Mon–Khmer and Munda divisions are debated, with some theories challenging the Mon–Khmer grouping and proposing additional potential branches.

Subdivisions of the Austroasiatic Language Family:

Munda Languages: The Munda languages are spoken by about nine million people in India and Bangladesh. Historically known as Kolarian languages, they are a branch of the Austroasiatic family, distinct from languages like Mon, Khmer, and Vietnamese. The Munda languages are divided into:

- **North Munda**: Includes languages such as Santali (widely spoken and official in India), Mundari, Ho, Korku, and Sora.
- **South Munda**: Spoken in central Odisha and along the Andhra Pradesh-Odisha border.

Characteristics:

- Three grammatical numbers (singular, dual, plural)
- Two genders (animate, inanimate)
- Distinction between inclusive and exclusive first person plural pronouns
- Use of suffixes or auxiliaries to indicate tense
- Polysynthetic and agglutinating structures
- Consonant sequences are rare except within words

Khasi-Palaungic Languages: This branch is classified by Sidwell (2011, 2018) as separate from the previous Khasi-Khmuic classification.

- **Khasic**: Includes languages such as Khasi, War, Lyngngam.
- **Palaungic**: Includes languages such as Palaung, Riang, Blang, Wa.

Khmuic Languages: Khmuic languages are spoken primarily in northern Laos, northern Vietnam, and southern Yunnan, China. Khmu is the most widely spoken language in this group.

- **Homeland**: Oudomxay Province, northern Laos.

Mang Languages: Mang languages are spoken in Vietnam, China, and Laos. Mang was first documented in 1974 and is spoken mainly in Lai Châu Province, Vietnam, and Jinping County, China.

- **Alternative Names**: Chaman, Abi, Mengga, Bageran, Mo (in China, classified as ethnic Bulang).

Pakanic Languages: Pakanic includes two languages: Bolyu and Bugan, spoken in Guangxi and Yunnan, China.

- **Historical Classifications**: Various proposals had included Mang, but it is now considered a separate branch.

Vietic Languages: The Vietic branch includes languages spoken by the Vietic peoples in Laos and Vietnam.

- **Languages**: Includes Vietnamese and Mường among others.
- **Significant Influences**: Vietnamese has a large stock of borrowed Chinese vocabulary and a significant Sino-Vietnamese influence.

Katuic Languages: Spoken by about 1.3 million people in Southeast Asia.

- **Geographic Distribution**: Includes languages in central Vietnam, Laos, and northeastern Cambodia.
- **Bahnaric Languages:** About 30 languages spoken by approximately 700,000 people in Vietnam, Cambodia, and Laos.

- **Geographic Distribution**: Central and southern Vietnam, eastern Cambodia, and parts of Laos.
- **Khmer Languages:** The official language of Cambodia, spoken by the Khmer people.
- **Dialects**: Includes Central Khmer, Northern Khmer (in Thailand), Southern Khmer (in Vietnam), and others in the Cardamom Mountains.

Characteristics:

- Analytic and isolating language
- No inflections or conjugations
- Written in the Khmer script, an abugida derived from Brahmi

Pearic Languages: A group of endangered languages spoken by Pear people in western Cambodia and eastern Thailand.

- **Languages**: Includes Por, Samré, Samray, Suoy, Chong.

Monic Languages: Descended from the Old Monic language of the kingdom of Dvaravati.

- **Languages**: Includes Mon and Nyahkur (a continuation of the Dvaravati kingdom).

Aslian Languages: Spoken on the Malay Peninsula by the Orang Asli.

- **Languages**:
  - **Jahaic ("Northern Aslian")**: Cheq Wong, Ten'edn (Mos), Batek, Jahai, Minriq.
  - **Senoic ("Central Aslian")**: Semai, Temiar, Lanoh.
  - **Southern Aslian (Semelaic)**: Mah Meri, Semelai, Temoq, Semaq Beri.

Origin: Originally appeared on the western side of the Malay Peninsula, spreading eastwards.

Nicobarese Languages: An isolated group of Austroasiatic languages spoken in the Nicobar Islands, India.

- **Languages**:
    - ♦ **Northern**: Car
    - ♦ **Central**: Nancowry, Camorta, Katchal
    - ♦ **Southern**: Sambelong, Shompen

Note: The Nicobarese languages are considered to subgroup with Aslian by some researchers.

These subdivisions reflect the diverse linguistic landscape within the Austroasiatic family, illustrating its complex structure and wide geographic distribution.

3. Tibetian – Burman Language Family:

The Tibeto-Burman (TB) languages form a diverse and extensive family spoken across the Himalayan region and parts of Southeast Asia. Here's a more detailed breakdown of this language family:

Overview of Tibeto-Burman Language Family

1. **Geographical Distribution:**
    - **Himalayan Region:** From Kashmir in the west to Tibet and across the Himalayan and sub-Himalayan regions of India, Nepal, Bhutan, Bangladesh, and China.
    - **Southeast Asia:** Extending into Burma (Myanmar), Thailand, Laos, and Vietnam.
    - **Total Number of Languages:** Several hundred, with some yet to be identified.
2. **Major Classifications:**
    - **Shafer (1974):** Four main groups:
        - ♦ **Bodic**
        - ♦ **Baric**
        - ♦ **Burmic**
        - ♦ **Karenic**
    - **Benedict (1972):** Eight subgroups plus an 'other' category, later reclassified into three groups by Benedict (1976).

3. Main Groups and Subgroups:

A. North-Eastern India Group:

- **Shafer's Baric Group:** Also known as Benedict's Bodo-Garo-Konyak group, now typically called the Sal group. Includes:
    - Jinghpaw (Kachin)
    - Sak or Luish Group
- **Characteristics:** Some lexical peculiarities, relatively simple tonal systems, and some morphology.

B. Western Group:

- **Shafer's Bodic Group & Benedict's Tibetan-Kanauri Group:**
    - **Bodic Subgroups:**
        - **Tibetan Proper**
        - **Western Bodish (e.g., Gurung, Tamang)**
        - **Eastern Bodish or Monpa**
        - **Kanauri (West Himalayish)**
    - **Himalayan Subgroups:**
        - **Kiranti (e.g., Rai)**
        - **Western Subgroup (e.g., Newari, Chepang)**

C. North-Eastern India Group (Central):

- **Core North-Eastern or Qiang Subgroup:**
    - **Characteristics:** Substantial shared verb morphology, mostly tonal.
    - **Languages:** Nungish, Naxi.

D. South-Eastern Group:

- **Shafer's Kukish & Benedict's Kuki-Chin-(Southern) Naga:**
    - **Languages:** Burmese-Lolo Subgroup, Karen Subgroup.
    - **Characteristics:** Complex tonal systems, minimal morphology, and SVO syntax in Karen. Bai also exhibits SVO syntax influenced by Chinese.

4. **Western Tibeto-Burman (Bodic):**
   - **Bodish Subgroup:**
     - **Tibetan Proper:** Includes various regional and local varieties.
     - **West Bodish:** Gurung, Tamang, Thakali, Manang, Kaike, Ghale.
     - **East Bodish:** Tshangla Group.
5. **Tibetan Varieties:**
   - **Central Bodish (Tibetan):** Various subgroups like Western, Central, Southern, Amdo, and Kharns.
     - **Regions:** Tibet, Ladakh, Bhutan, Nepal, northernmost Burma.
     - **Population:** Approximately 4.9 million speakers (including both Tibetan proper and related groups).
6. **Western Tibetan:**
   - **Languages:**
     - **Balti:** Spoken in Baltistan, written in Arabic script.
     - **Ladakhi:** Spoken in Ladakh; also known as Ladwags.
     - **Zangskar:** Distinct dialect in Zangskar Valley.

Key Points:

- The Tibeto-Burman languages are rich in diversity, with various languages exhibiting unique phonological, morphological, and syntactic features.
- There are ongoing efforts to map and classify these languages, as well as to document those that are endangered.

This summary provides a glimpse into the complexity and breadth of the Tibeto-Burman language family, illustrating its importance across a vast geographical and cultural landscape.

Western Subgroup:

- **Lahuli Varieties:** Spoken by about 25,000 people in Lahul. These include Tod and Ranglo, also known as Khoksar. Tod is spoken in the Tod valley by around 1,700 people, and

Ranglo is spoken by about 1,000 people in four villages north of the Rohtang Pass. These varieties are sometimes confused with other local languages.

- **Piti (Spiti):** Spoken by over 12,000 people in the Spiti valley. It includes dialects like Tod, Bhar, Pin, and Sham.
- **mNyam and mNyamskad:** mNyam is spoken in the Spiti valley, while mNyamskad or Nyarnkat is spoken in Kanaur with fewer speakers.
- **Jad Variety:** Also known as Garhwal Bhotia, this variety is underenumerated with a few hundred speakers. It should not be confused with Rangkhas, another West Himalayish language spoken by the Rangpa or Marchha people.
- **mNgahris Subgroup:** Found mostly in Ngari (Chinese Ali) Prefecture in western Tibet, extending into north-western Nepal. Includes varieties like Ruthog, sGar, rTsamdah, sPuhreng, mTshochen, dGergyas, and a seventh in western Shigatse Prefecture. The total number of speakers is around 40,000.

Gtsang Subgroup:

- **Northern Nepal Varieties:** Includes Dolpo, Reng Pungmo, and Tichurong in the Dolpo region, and bKag and gLo in Mustang. Nar, Gyasumdo, Nubri, and Tsum are spoken north of the Gurung area, with about 3,200 Nubri and Tsum speakers.
- **Sherpa:** Over 70,000 speakers, mostly in north-eastern Nepal, with smaller populations in China and India. Kagate is a related language spoken south of the Sherpa area.
- **Jirel, Lhomi, and Halung:** Jirel (3,000 speakers), Lhomi (4,000 speakers), and Halung (east of Lhomi) are spoken in north-eastern Nepal.
- **Gtsang Varieties in Tibet:** Includes sKyidgrong, Dingri, gZhiskartse (Shigatse), rGyalrtse (Gyantse), and sNadkarrtse. Total speakers in China are nearly 460,000.

Dbus (Central Tibetan):

- **Lhasa:** The 'standard' variety of Tibetan with about 450,000 speakers. It includes various other dialects like Chushur, hPhanpo, rTsethang, and hLunrtse. It is widely spoken by Tibetan refugees, with about 150,000 refugees globally, mainly in India and Nepal.

Southern Tibetan:

- **Tromowa (Gromo):** Spoken in the Chumbi valley between Sikkim and Bhutan.
- **Danjong (ka):** Spoken by over 70,000 people in Sikkim and used in education. A modified Tibetan script is used.
- **Dzongkba (Drukpa):** The Tibetan variety of western Bhutan, with about 225,000 speakers. Dzongkha has become the national language of Bhutan.

Amdo (Northeastern Tibetan):

- **Varieties:** Known for their archaic features, including nasal prefixes. Includes Golok, hBrogpa, Rongba, and rTahu. Total speakers are about 810,000. Notable varieties include Braghgo and rTahu.

Khams (Southeastern Tibetan):

- **Western Khams:** Includes rGer-rtse in Ngari Prefecture, with about 160,000 speakers.
- **Eastern Khams:** Extends over a large area with about 960,000 speakers, including varieties like sDege, dKarmdzes, Chabmdo, Braggyab, Nyingkhri, h8ahthang, and Nyagchu.
- **Northern Khams:** Includes hBristod, Khrihdu, sKyergu(mdo), and Nangchen, with about 91,000 speakers.
- **Southern Khams:** Includes varieties like sDerong, bDechen, rGyalthang, and Phyaphreng, with about 135,000 speakers.
- **Cone Khams:** Spoken by about 77,000 people, separated from other Khams varieties by the Amdo-speaking area.

- **bBrugchu:** The easternmost Khams variety with about 30,000 speakers.

West Bodish (Gurung, Tamang) Group:

- **Kutang Ghale:** Spoken by about 1,300 people in the Kutang area, linguistically closer to Ghale.
- **Ghale:** About 15,000 speakers in 33 villages. Shows Tibetan linguistic influence.
- **Kaike:** Spoken by about 2,000 people, sometimes known as Tarali Kham.
- **Gurung:** Spoken by approximately 150,000 people. Has two major dialects, west and east, with significant differences.
- **Thakali:** Spoken by about 5,000 people, also known as Tapaang. Includes closely related Panchgaon people.
- **Chantel:** Spoken by part of a group in Myagdi; limited linguistic data available.
- **Rohani:** Small group to the south of Thakali and west of Gurung, with unclear classification.
- **Manang:** Spoken by about 3,000 people with Tibetan influence.
- **Tamang:** Spoken by around 600,000 people with significant dialectal diversity.

The East Bodish and Himalayan language groups represent a fascinating array of languages and dialects found in the northeastern regions of India, Bhutan, and Tibet. Here's a summary of the East Bodish and Himalayan language groups based on the information provided:

East Bodish Group:

A. Dzalakha:

- **Location**: North-eastern Bhutan, Tawang District in Arunachal Pradesh, India, and adjacent areas of Tibet (Cuona region).

- **Speakers**: Approximately 15,000 in Bhutan, 30,000 in India, and 7,000 in Tibet.
- **Variants**: Central Monpa (India), Cuona Menba (Tibet).

B. **East Monpa:**

- **Location**: North-central Arunachal Pradesh and adjacent areas in Tibet.
- **Speakers**: Around 5,000.
- **Terminology**: Also known as Motuo Menba in China.

C. **Sherdukpen:**

- **Location**: South-eastern part of West Kameng District, Arunachal Pradesh.
- **Speakers**: About 4,000.
- **Subgroups**: Bot (centered around Bot village) and Lish.

D. **Lhokpu and Gongduk:**

- **Location**: South-western and south-central Bhutan, respectively.
- **Lhokpu**: Also known as Lhobikha.
- **Gongduk**: Also known as Gongdubikha.
- **Cultural Note**: These languages might represent the autochthonous groups of the area before Tibetan migrations.

Tshangla and East Bodish:

A. **Tshangla:**

- **Location**: South-eastern Bhutan and western West Kameng District of Arunachal Pradesh.
- **Speakers**: Tshangla served as a lingua franca among various Monpa groups.
- **Alternate Name**: Sharchop ('eastern people').

B. **Lhokpu:**

- **Location**: South-western Bhutan.
- **Alternate Name**: Lhobikha.

C. **Gongduk:**

- **Location**: South-central Bhutan.
- **Alternate Name**: Gongdubikha.

West Himalayish:

A. **Pattani:**

- **Location**: Along the Chandra (upper Chinab) River, northern Himachal Pradesh.
- **Speakers**: About 20,000.
- **Variants**: Chamba Lahuli (6,000 speakers).

B. **Tinan (Gondhla):**

- **Location**: South of the Chandra River, near its junction with the Bhaga River.
- **Speakers**: About 2,500.

C. **Bunan (Ga(h)ri):**

- **Location**: Along the Bhaga River, western Lahul.
- **Speakers**: About 5,000.

D. **Kanauri (Kinnauri):**

- **Location**: Kinnaur area.
- **Speakers**: About 60,000.
- **Variants**: Lower and upper Kanauri, Thebor or Thebar, and Chitkbuli.

E. **Kanashi:**

- **Location**: Malana village, near Kulu.
- **Speakers**: About 1,100.

F. **Rangpa:**

- **Location**: North-central Garhwal, Uttar Pradesh.
- **Speakers**: Estimated 7,500.
- **Linguistic Note**: Rangpa is used as a collective term for various Hinduised non-Tibetan TB groups.

G. Thami:

- **Location**: Eastern Nepal.
- **Speakers**: About 14,000.

Himalayan Languages:

- **Classification**: Includes nearly all non-Tibetan TB languages of Nepal.
- **General Features**: Tibetan-derived groups inhabit the northern quarter of Nepal, while Indic groups inhabit the southern quarter.
- **Migration Impact**: Extensive migration has spread Nepali northward and eastward, while Tibetan groups have also migrated outside their traditional areas but predominantly speak Nepali.

These diverse languages reflect a rich tapestry of linguistic and cultural interactions in the region.

This extensive text provides an overview of the languages spoken in the Central Himalayan and North-East Indian regions, categorizing them into various groups and subgroups. Here's a summary and key points for each category:

Central Himalayan Languages:

A. Magar:

- **Location:** Lower hills in western Nepal.
- **Speakers:** Estimated 290,000 by van Driem; many now speak other languages like Kham.
- **Notes:** Magar was historically the language of a major kingdom. Further research is needed to distinguish it from Raute and Raji.

B. Raute and Raji:

- **Location:** Western Nepal and adjacent India.
- **Notes:** Raute and Raji are small nomadic groups. Raji may be a Munda language with significant Tibeto-Burman and Indic contact.

C. **Kham:**

- **Location:** Nepal.
- **Speakers:** About 40,000.
- **Notes:** Language is distinct from Magar despite some overlaps.

D. **Chepang:**

- **Location:** Nepal.
- **Speakers:** About 17,000.
- **Notes:** Includes some nomadic Bankariya. Detailed studies have been conducted.

E. **Newari:**

- **Location:** Kathmandu Valley, Nepal.
- **Speakers:** Approximately 600,000.
- **Notes:** Major language with a rich history and literature, though the status has declined. Newari literature is flourishing in modern Devanagari script.

Kiranti or Rai Languages:

A. **General Overview:**

- **Location:** Eastern Nepal.
- **Speakers:** Approximately 400,000, though many have shifted to Nepali.
- **Notes:** Rai languages are endangered and need further research.

B. **Subgroups and Languages:**

- **Sunwar, Yakkha, Limbu:** Part of the Rai group with substantial speakers.
- **Khaling:** About 12,000 speakers.
- **Dumi and Kohi:** Small groups with few speakers.
- **Bantawa:** Widespread and dialectally diverse.
- **Chamling:** Fairly numerous and widely scattered.

- **Belhare, Chintang, Chulung:** Small languages, some in the process of extinction.
- **Yakkha and Mewahang:** Large languages with dialectal variations.

North-East Indian/Sal Languages:

A. Overview:

- **Characteristics:** Noted for innovative etyma such as *sal for 'sun'.
- **Subgroups:**
    - **Shafer's Baric Group:** Includes languages like Boro, Dimas(a), Kokborok, Garo, and more.
    - **Jinghpaw (Kachin):** Central nucleus of TB languages.
    - **Luish (Sak):** Scattered and moribund languages.
    - **Pyu:** Extinct language of central Burma.

B. Languages and Dialects:

- **Boro:** Widely spoken in north-eastern India with a significant number of speakers.
- **Garo:** Spoken in Meghalaya, with about half a million speakers.
- **Kokborok:** Also known as Tripuri, with substantial speakers in Tripura.
- **Dimasa:** Spoken in North Cachar Hills with around 150,000 members.
- **Rabha:** Scattered in the Brahmaputra valley with about 50,000 speakers.
- **Hajong:** Small language with limited linguistic data.

Northern Naga Languages:

A. Overview:

- **Characteristics:** Part of the Baric subgroup with diverse and complex subgroupings.
- **Languages and Groups:**
    - ♦ **Khienmungan, Chang, Ao, Konyak, Phom, Wancho:** Various groups with differing numbers of speakers and linguistic descriptions.
    - ♦ **Nocte and Tangsa:** Significant languages in India and Burma with multiple dialects.

The study provides an intricate picture of the linguistic diversity in these regions, highlighting the need for ongoing research and preservation efforts, especially for endangered languages.

This study provides an overview of several linguistic and ethnic groups in the regions of Burma (Myanmar), India, and China. Here's a summary:

Jinghpaw (Singpho, Kachin):

- **Population**: Estimated 0.9 million, with over 600,000 speaking Jinghpaw as their first language.
- **Geographic Distribution**: Northern Burma, parts of China (Jingpo nationality), and India.
- **Dialects**: Includes the Gauri (Kauri, Hkauri) dialect and other minor dialects.
- **Language Status**: Widely used with a roman orthography that does not indicate tones. Developing separate roman orthographies for some Burmish languages.

Sak or Luish Group:

- **Kadu**: Moribund with about 20,000 speakers; related to the Kantu from the Tagaung kingdom.
- **Ganan**: Spoken by about 7,000 people.
- **Taman**: Fewer than 1,000 speakers; closely related to Malin, Andro, and related languages.

- **Sak (Thet, Arakanese That)**: Around 7,000 speakers, with a presence in Burma and Bangladesh.

Pyu:

- **Historical Context**: Ancient kingdom in central Burma, known for irrigated agriculture and major centers like Halin and Sriksetra.
- **Language**: Extinct but known from inscriptions. The Pyu script is the earliest script for a Tibeto-Burman language.

Kuki-Chin:

- **Overview**: A cohesive subgroup with extensive research showing links to Burmic and Burmese-Lolo.
- **Geographic Distribution**: India (Nagaland, Manipur, Mizoram), Burma (Chin State).
- **Subgroups**: Includes Kuki, Chin, and various Naga groups.
- **Languages**: Features tone languages with extensive verb morphology. Notable groups include Thado (Kuki), Zeliangrong, and Meithei (Manipuri).

Southern Naga:

- **Languages**: Includes Ao (about 110,000 speakers), Sangtam (30,000), Rengma (15,000), Lhota (60,000), Yimchunger (30,000), Maring (15,000), and Serna (100,000).
- **Characteristics**: Diverse group with roman orthographies for many languages. Linguistic similarities among some groups.

Kuki:

- **Overview**: Refers to various small groups around the Manipur valley, including Rangkhol, Bete, Hallam, Langrong, and others.
- **Population**: Over 20,000 speakers of different Kuki languages.

- **Languages**: Includes Hmar, Anal, Chawte, Mayol, Lamgang, Kom, and others. Some languages have been replaced by Meithei.

The document highlights the complexity and diversity of Tibeto-Burman languages and ethnic groups in this region, reflecting a rich tapestry of linguistic and cultural heritage.

Chin: It is a study of the North Chin, Central Chin, South Chin, and other Chin groups mentioned:

North Chin:

- **Overview**: Includes significant groups like the Thado(u) and several other 'Kuki' groups.
- **Speakers**: Over 250,000 across Manipur, adjacent areas, and Burma.
- **Languages**: Includes Thado(u) (50,000), Chiru (5,000), Gangte (7,000), Pawi (10,000), Simte (5,000). In Burma, notable subgroups are Thado, Siyin, Paite, Vuite, Sokte, Karnhau.
- **Orthographies**: Roman orthographies are in use for most languages.

Central Chin:

- **Overview**: Known collectively as Laizo, includes a wide range of dialects with significant diversity.
- **Languages**: Includes Mizo (formerly Lushai) and other dialects such as Bawm (6,000), Paangkhua (3,000), Zahao, Tashon, Ngawn, Zanniat, Zophei, Lawtu, Lailen, Senthang, Tawr, and more.
- **Speakers**: About 400,000 in Burma, 10,000 in Bangladesh, with substantial populations in Mizoram (India). Mizo is the largest group with around 400,000 speakers.
- **Orthographies**: Roman orthographies are used for many dialects; Mizo is widely used in its roman form.

South Chin:

- **Overview**: Diverse group with various names and significant regional variations.
- **Languages**: Includes Khyang (Bangladesh), Zolarnnai, Welaung, Matu, M'kang, Ng'men, Nitu (Daai), Hngizung, Utpu, Chinbok (Saingbaung Chin), Asho Chin.
- **Speakers**: Over 250,000 in Burma, with some in the plains no longer speaking Chin. Nitu has about 30,000 speakers.

Other Chin Groups:

- **Khami/Khumi**: Includes dialects in Burma and Bangladesh, with a roman orthography in use.
    - **Speakers**: Around 50,000 in Burma and several thousand in Bangladesh.
- **Mara (Lakher/Maram)**: Known as Lakher (Central Chin name) and Maram (from their own name). About 20,000 speakers, mostly in India.
- **Arleng/Karbi/Mikir**: A widespread language with various dialects such as Amri, Bhoi, and Renglchang.
    - **Speakers**: Estimates vary from 200,000 to 600,000, with many Arleng speakers now using Assamese.
    - **Autonym**: Officially known as Karbi, but the main autonym is Arleng.

This summary highlights the diversity and distribution of Chin languages, including their various names, populations, and linguistic characteristics.

Central Tibeto-Burman:

The classification of Central Tibeto-Burman languages is complex and still debated, primarily due to a lack of comprehensive data. The languages are spoken in northeastern India, northern Burma, and adjacent regions of northwestern Yunnan and southeastern Tibet. They are influenced by Tibetan from the north and Assamese from the southwest.

Major Clusters:

A. West Arunachal Languages

- **Sulung (Puroik)**: Former slaves of dominant groups, poorly described language. Population around 1,516 (1961 census), though estimates suggest more, including some in Tibet.
- **Bugun (Kboa/Khowa)**: About 1,700 speakers, culturally influenced by the Monpa. Limited linguistic data.
- **Hruso (Aka/Angka)**: About 4,000 speakers, poorly described language.
- **Dhammai (Miji)**: About 5,000 speakers, culturally similar to Hruso but with limited linguistic data.
- **Bangru**: Small group of about 1,000 in Tibet and Arunachal Pradesh. Limited information available.

B. Adi-Mising-Nishi (Abor-Miri-Dafla), Misingish or Tani Group

- **Nishi (Bangni, Apa Tani, Tagen/Tagin)**: Approximately 170,000 speakers, with some in Tibet. Known collectively as Dafla, now replaced by various subgroup names.
- **Hill Miri**: Small group in central Arunachal Pradesh, closely related to Nishi.
- **Adi (Abor)**: Large group with various subgroups like Gallong (Galo), Bokar (Bogar), Pailibo, Bori, Ashing, Tangam, Shimong, Minyong, Milang, Pasi, Panggi, Padam. Over 125,000 speakers, with some extending into Tibet.
- **Mising**: Scattered in the upper Brahmaputra valley and northern hills, with an estimated 500,000 members. Not all speak the language. Romanization developed but not approved for educational use.

C. Digarish 'Mishmi'

- **Idu**: About 20,000 speakers, two-thirds in Arunachal Pradesh, the rest in Tibet. Included with the Luoba nationality in Tibet.

- **Taraon 'Mishmi'**: Also known as Tain, Taying, or Darang Deng. About 12,000 speakers, mostly in India, with fewer in Tibet and northern Burma.

D. Keman 'Mishmi'

- **Keman (Geman Deng, Miju Mishmi)**: About 20,000 speakers, two-thirds in Arunachal Pradesh, the rest in Tibet.

Lepcha:

- **Overview**: Known as Rong to its speakers, Lepcha was traditionally spoken in Sikkim, parts of Darjeeling, and southwestern Bhutan. Current speaker population is around 4,000, with a total ethnic population of 26,000 in India and 2,000 in Bhutan.
- **Script**: Traditional script, efforts have been made to teach it in schools. Described in early works by Mainwaring (1876) and Sprigg (1983).

The Central Tibeto-Burman languages encompass a range of languages spoken in north eastern India, northern Burma, and adjacent regions. The classification of these languages is complex, with various groups and subgroups, each with distinct linguistic and cultural characteristics.

Rawang/Nungish Languages:

Overview: The Rawang/Nungish languages are a large and diverse group within the Tibeto-Burman language family. These languages are spoken primarily in northern Burma and south awestern China, including parts of Tibet. The classification and terminology used for these languages are complex and have evolved over time.

A. Historical Background and Classification:

- The term "Rawang" originally referred to a large super group within the Nungish languages but is now used more broadly to describe the entire group.

- "Nung" is the Jinghpaw name for this group and serves as the basis for terms used by scholars such as Benedict and Shafer.
- Former Chinese names include Nuzi, Luzi, and Jiuzi.

B. Geographical Distribution:

- **Burma**: Approximately 150,000 speakers.
- **China**: About 25,000 speakers, including those classified under the Dulong and Nu nationalities.

C. Major Clusters:

- **Mvtwang Clan Cluster**: The largest cluster with around 50,000 speakers. It serves as the basis for the standard Rawang orthography.
- **Dulong Clan Cluster**: Includes about 11,000 speakers. The Dulong clan is part of the Nu nationality in China and includes several distinct dialects.
- **Dvru (Daru) Clan Cluster**: About 35,000 speakers in Burma.
- **Anung Clan Cluster**: Mainly in China with about 6,000 speakers. It includes a few in Burma.
- **Nusu**: Over 8,000 speakers in China with significant internal dialectal differences.
- **Dvngsar (Tangsarr)**: Around 15,000 speakers.
- **Lungmi (Longmi)**: Southernmost clan with nearly 30,000 speakers, influenced by Jinghpaw.

D. Dialects and Orthographies:

- The Mvtwang dialect has been chosen as the standard for Rawang, with a romanization system used among Christians in Burma.
- In China, Dulong has a pinyin orthography, while Anung has a roman script used in religious texts.
- Dialects within the Rawang/Nungish group can vary significantly.

North-Eastern Tibeto-Burman Languages:

Overview: This group of languages includes various Tibeto-Burman languages spoken in north-eastern China, north-western Yunnan, and adjacent regions. The exact classification of these languages is still debated, with some proposing they form a subgroup called Qiangic.

Key Points:

A. **Core Qiangic Languages:**
- **Qiang**: Recognized as a separate nationality in China, with two distinct dialects. The northern dialect is non-tonal, while the southern dialect is tonal.
- **Pumi**: Another separate nationality with significant population estimates, though census figures are low. It is closely related to Qiang.
- **Baima, Jiarong, Ergong, Zaba, Guichong, Ersu, Choyo, Namuyi, Muya, Shixing**: Various languages within this group with varying speaker numbers and characteristics. Pinyin orthography exists for Qiang, but no other core Qiangic languages have an orthography.

B. **Other North-Eastern Tibeto-Burman Languages:**
- **Naxi**: Transitional between Qiangic and Bunnic, with a traditional pictographic writing system. About 210,000 speakers, with Moso as a distinct language.
- **Tujia**: Spoken by about 170,000 people. The language has numerous Chinese loanwords and is spoken mainly by older individuals.
- **Bai**: Spoken by over a million people, with a long history and significant Chinese influence. It has been described as having extensive borrowings from Chinese dialects. Bai's classification within Tibeto-Burman is debated, and it is sometimes considered a Chinese dialect.

- The Rawang/Nungish and North-Eastern Tibeto-Burman languages are complex and diverse, with various dialects and classifications. The Rawang/Nungish languages include a large number of subgroups and dialects across Burma and China, while the North-Eastern Tibeto-Burman languages include several distinct languages with debated classifications and varying degrees of influence from neighboring languages and cultures.

Xixia (Tangut):

Overview: The Xixia, also known as Tangut, were a people who founded the Xixia Kingdom, which existed from around 990 AD until its fall in 1227 AD. The kingdom's capital was located in what is now Ningxia. The Xixia language and script are significant due to their historical and linguistic features.

Historical Context:

- **Kingdom Establishment**: The Xixia Kingdom was established around 990 AD, with the most commonly accepted historical date being 1032 AD.
- **Conquest and Fall**: The kingdom was conquered by Genghis Khan's forces in 1227 AD. During the siege, Genghis Khan died, and his forces eventually destroyed the city and massacred its inhabitants.
- **Marco Polo's Account**: Marco Polo, in his writings, referred to the Xixia people as Tangut and mentioned their language and culture.

Writing System:

- **Creation**: The Xixia script was devised around 1037 AD by Li Yuanhao, a Xixia scholar familiar with Chinese characters. This script predates the Burmese script and the old Newar script.
- **Characteristics**: The script's phonetic values are uncertain. Existing Xixia texts, primarily translations from Chinese,

have been partially understood due to an 1190 Xixia-Chinese dictionary.

Linguistic Classification:

- **Phonetic Value**: There are competing theories regarding the phonetic value of the Xixia script. These include a Russian theory, a Chinese theory, and the work of Nishida. Kwanten's claims that Xixia was not Tibeto-Burman and his alternative ideas about the phonetic value of the script have been contested.
- **Tibeto-Burman Affiliation**: Some aspects of Xixia phonology and lexicon suggest it was part of the North-eastern Tibeto-Burman group, though its exact classification remains debated.

Significance:

- The Xixia language and script are crucial for understanding the historical and linguistic landscape of the Tibeto-Burman family. The surviving texts and inscriptions provide insights into the Xixia culture and their interactions with neighboring cultures, including Chinese.

The Xixia or Tangut were an influential group with a distinct language and writing system that have intrigued historians and linguists. Despite the kingdom's fall and the destruction of its capital, the legacy of the Xixia script and language continues to be a subject of scholarly interest and debate.

South-Eastern Tibeto-Burman:

The South-Eastern Tibeto-Burman (TB) languages are a diverse group comprising several subgroups, including Burmese-Lolo, Mru, and Ugong. Each of these subgroups exhibits unique linguistic features and is geographically dispersed across different regions.

Burmese-Lolo:

Description: Burmese-Lolo (BL), also referred to as Lolo-Burmese or Burmese-Yipho, is a large and varied branch of Tibeto-Burman. It is traditionally divided into two main subgroups:

A. **Burmish:** This includes Burmese and its related languages.

B. **Loloish:** This subgroup encompasses a variety of languages spoken in southern China and northern Southeast Asia.

A third subgroup, **Ugong**, is considered to be intermediate between the Burmish and Loloish subgroups. The Burmese-Lolo languages are characterized by their verb-final structure, complex tonal systems, and significant initial consonant clusters, with relatively little inflectional morphology.

- **Burmish**: Includes Burmese, the official language of Myanmar, and other related languages.
- **Loloish**: Encompasses languages spoken in parts of China, including the Yi languages, which are grouped under Loloish.

Linguistic Features:

- **Verb-Final**: The basic word order is subject-object-verb (SOV).
- **Tonal Systems**: Complex systems of tonal distinctions.
- **Morphology**: Limited or no inflectional morphology.

Mru:

Description: Mru is spoken by about 40,000 people, primarily in Arakan State of Myanmar and some areas of Bangladesh. Its classification within Tibeto-Burman is uncertain, and it shows significant contact influence from Kuki-Chin languages and Burmese.

- **Position in TB**: Mru may be remotely related to the Burmese-Lolo group, though its exact classification remains debated. Some scholars, including Loffier and Shafer, suggest a distant relationship with Burmese-Lolo.

Linguistic Features:

- **Contact Influence**: The language exhibits vocabulary borrowings from Kuki-Chin languages and Burmese.

Ugong:

Description: The Ugong language is spoken by a small and diminishing population of around 300 speakers in western central Thailand. Most Ugong speakers are bilingual in Thai, and younger members of the community are semi-speakers of Ugong.

- **Current Status**: The language is no longer spoken in many of its former locations and is at risk of extinction.

Linguistic Features:

- **Language Shift**: Ugong is largely replaced by Thai among younger speakers, leading to its endangerment.

The South-Eastern Tibeto-Burman languages represent a significant and diverse branch of the Tibeto-Burman family. They include a range of languages with distinct characteristics and varying degrees of endangerment. The Burmese-Lolo languages are prominent for their verb-final structure and complex tonal systems, while Mru and Ugong contribute unique linguistic features and show varying levels of interaction with neighbouring languages.

It is a concise study of the information you provided on the Tibeto-Burman (TB) languages:

Burmish:

- **Burmese**:
  - **Speakers**: ~32 million (first language); ~10 million (second language).
  - **Dialects**: Includes Arakanese (Mogh/Magh), Tavoyan, Beik, Intha, Danu, Taungyo, and Yaw.
  - **Status**: National language of Myanmar (Burma), with various regional dialects and a significant literature.
- **Other Burmish Languages**:
  - **Achang**: ~30,000 speakers, integrated with Kachin or Shan cultures.
  - **Lashi**: ~30,000 speakers, primarily in Burma.

- **Maru**: ~100,000 speakers, dispersed, operates within Kachin culture.
- **Atsi**: ~150,000 speakers, with distinctive phonological features.
- **Phun (Hpun)**: Moribund, with a few hundred speakers remaining.

Loloish Languages:

- **Northern Loloish**:
  - **Nosu**: ~2 million speakers, in southern Sichuan and north-western Yunnan.
  - **Nasu**: ~850,000 speakers, spread over Guizhou, Yunnan, and Guangxi.
  - **Small Groups**: Includes Laka (~30,000), Kepo (~90,000), Sani (~10,000), Sangwie (~20,000), and others.
- **Central Loloish**:
  - **Languages**: Includes Sani, Axi, Azhe, Azha.
  - **Speakers**: ~400,000, mainly in south-eastern Yunnan.
- **Southern Loloish**:
  - **Akoid**:
    - **Akha**: ~550,000 speakers across northern Thailand, Laos, China, and Burma.
    - **Hani**: ~520,000 speakers in southern Yunnan, with some in Vietnam.
    - **Haoni & Baihong**: Smaller groups within the Hani cluster.
- **Biska**:
  - **Biyue & Kaduo**: ~300,000 speakers in southern Yunnan and northern Laos.
  - **Mpi**: ~1,500 speakers in northern Thailand.
- **Bisoid**:
  - **Bisu**: ~500 speakers in Thailand, with dialects in different villages.

- ♦ **Phunoi (C6ng)**: ~30,000 speakers in Laos and Vietnam.

Karen Languages:

- **General Characteristics**:
  - ♦ **Word Order**: SVO (Subject-Verb-Object), unique in TB.
  - ♦ **Population**: ~2.5 to 4 million including Burma and Thailand.
- **Major Groups**:
  - ♦ **Sgaw**: ~1.6 million speakers, including diverse dialects.
  - ♦ **Pho (Pwo)**: ~1.4 million speakers, with dialects across southern Burma and Thailand.
  - ♦ **Kayah (Kayaw)**: ~250,000 speakers, including various dialects like Manu and Yintale.
  - ♦ **Bwe**: Central Karen with ~25,000 speakers, also known as Blimaw.
  - ♦ **Gebas**: ~10,000 speakers.

Conclusion:

The TB languages consist of about 250 languages, with around 65 million speakers. Burmese is the most spoken TB language, accounting for a significant portion of these speakers. Efforts are ongoing to document and preserve endangered languages within this diverse family.

This overview covers the main language groups and notable languages within the South-Eastern Tibeto-Burman languages, illustrating their distribution and linguistic features.

4. Tai Kadai/Kra-Dai/DaicKadai and Language Group:

The Kra-Dai (also known as Tai-Kadai or Daic) language family encompasses a variety of languages spoken primarily in Southern China, Northeast India, and Southeast Asia. It's one of the major language families in the region, comprising close to 100 languages spoken by around 100 million people across China, Thailand, Laos, Myanmar, India, and Vietnam.

Branches and Languages: Kra-Dai is divided into two major groups:

A. **Tai (Kam-Tai):**
   - **Main Languages:** Thai (national language of Thailand), Lao (national language of Laos)
   - **Related Languages:** Zhuang (largest minority language in China), Kam, Sui, and others.
   - **Writing Systems:** Thai and Lao use Indic-based scripts; Zhuang and Kam-Sui use Chinese characters or Romanized scripts.

B. **Kadai:**
   - **Languages:** Includes lesser-known languages such as Gelao, Lachi, and Laqua (Qabiao).
   - **Writing Systems:** Most Kadai languages do not have their own writing systems, with some using Chinese characters or Romanized scripts.

Historical and Genetic Affiliation:

- **Historical Theories:**
  - ♦ Paul Benedict originally proposed the affiliation of Tai-Kadai with Austronesian, forming the Tai-Austronesian hypothesis.
  - ♦ James R. Chamberlain suggested that the Tai-Kadai family originated as early as the 12th century BCE in Southern China.
  - ♦ Weera Ostapirat supports the idea that Kra-Dai and Austronesian might be sister language families.
  - ♦ Laurent Sagart proposed that Kra-Dai could be a branch of Austronesian that migrated back to mainland China.
- **Current Theories:**
  - ♦ **Sino-Tai Hypothesis:** Suggests a connection between Tai and Sino-Tibetan languages.
  - ♦ **Austro-Tai Hypothesis:** Proposes a genetic link between Tai and Austronesian languages.

- **Sino - Tibetan - Austronesian Hypothesis:** Suggests a broader phylum that includes Tai-Kadai, Sino-Tibetan, Miao-Yao, and Austronesian.

Internal Classification: Kra-Dai languages are categorized into several branches:

A. **Tai:**
- **Location:** Southern China, Southeast Asia.
- **Subgroups:** Includes languages like Thai, Lao, and others.

B. **Kra:**
- **Location:** Southern China, Northern Vietnam.
- **Note:** Sometimes referred to as Kadai.

C. **Kam-Sui:**
- **Location:** Guizhou and Guangxi, China.

D. **Be:**
- **Location:** Hainan, possibly including Jizhao of Guangdong.

E. **Hlai:**
- **Location:** Hainan.

Unclassified or Mixed-Origin Languages:

- **Unclassified Languages:** Lakkia, Biao, Jiamao, Jizhao.
- **Mixed-Origin Languages:** Hezhang Buyi (Northern Tai and Kra), E (Northern Tai and Pinghua Chinese), Caolan (Northern Tai and Central Tai), Sanqiao (Kam-Sui, Hmongic, and Chinese), Jiamao (Hlai and other unknown elements).

Writing Systems:

- **Tai Languages:** Use Indic-based scripts (Thai, Lao) or Chinese characters (Zhuang, Kam-Sui).
- **Kadai Languages:** Primarily oral with some using Chinese characters or Romanized scripts.

Research and Controversies:

- The genetic affiliation of Tai-Kadai remains debated, with ongoing research needed to clarify relationships with other language families and within Kra-Dai itself. Evidence and theories continue to evolve, reflecting the complex history and diversity of these languages.

Andamanese Language Family

The Andamanese languages are spoken by the indigenous peoples of the Andaman Islands in the Indian Ocean. These languages are grouped into two known families: Great Andamanese and Ongan. There are also two unattested languages, Sentinelese and Jangil.

Classification:

A. Great Andamanese:

- **Languages:** Historically, the Great Andamanese family included ten distinct languages, but many have become extinct. The languages are: Aka-Bea, Akar-Bale, A-Pucikwar, Oko-Juwoi, Aka-Kol, Aka-Kede, Aka-Jeru, Aka-Bo, Aka-Kora, Aka-Cari
- **Current Status:** By the early 21st century, the Great Andamanese languages had largely disappeared. Only a small number of people speak a modified version called "Present Great Andamanese" or "Jero," mainly based on Aka-Jeru. Hindi is increasingly used as the primary language by the descendants.

B. Ongan:

- ♦ **Languages:**
- ♦ **Jarawa**
- ♦ **Onge**
- **Current Status:** Both languages are spoken by approximately 670 people. They have survived due to their relative isolation and resistance to outside contact.

C. **Unattested Languages:**

- **Sentinelese:**
    - ♦ **Current Status:** The Sentinelese people refuse contact with outsiders, so the language remains unknown. Estimates suggest there are between 50 to 250 speakers. Anvita Abbi (2020) believes Sentinelese might be related to Ongan.
- **Jangil:**
    - ♦ **Current Status:** Jangil is extinct, with the last known speakers having died in the 1920s. Maurice Vidal Portman noted similarities between Jangil and Jarawa, suggesting a possible relationship, but this remains unconfirmed.

Historical Context:

- **Early Records:** The indigenous peoples of the Andaman Islands had minimal contact with outside powers until the late 18th century, when the British established a colonial presence. By the 1860s, a penal colony was set up, leading to significant changes, including the introduction of mainland settlers and indentured labourers. This resulted in severe population decline and cultural disruptions among the Andamanese.
- **Linguistic Studies:** Early linguistic documentation was initiated by Alexander John Ellis, who studied South Andamanese languages and presented his findings to the Philological Society. This work contributed to the early understanding of the Andamanese languages.

Contemporary Status:

- **Great Andamanese:** The languages have largely become extinct due to historical disruptions, with only a modified version of the language and Hindi being used by the remaining descendants.

- **Ongan:** Jarawa and Onge languages have survived due to the isolation of their speakers and their resistance to contact with outsiders.
- **Sentinelese and Jangil:** The languages remain poorly understood due to the lack of direct contact with the Sentinelese and the extinction of Jangil.

Linguistic Relationships:

- **Great Andamanese vs. Ongan:** There is no conclusive evidence that Great Andamanese and Ongan languages are genealogically related. Typological similarities exist, but shared vocabulary is minimal. Scholars like Anvita Abbi and Radcliffe-Brown have debated the potential connections, with most consensus leaning towards the languages being unrelated.
- **Sentinelese Relationship:** The relationship between Sentinelese and other Andamanese languages remains speculative, with some scholars suggesting a potential link to Ongan based on linguistic features.

Key Points:

- The term "Andamanese languages" is a geographic label rather than a genetic one, as the languages within this category are not closely related.
- Historical contact and population decline have significantly impacted the linguistic diversity and preservation of Andamanese languages.
- Ongoing research and exploration are necessary to better understand the relationships and histories of these languages, especially the unattested ones.

State Official Languages of India

Andhra Pradesh:

Official Language: Telugu

- **Telugu:** Telugu is a Dravidian language native to the Indian states of Andhra Pradesh and Telangana, where it serves as the official language. Spoken by about 96 million people, Telugu is the most widely spoken member of the Dravidian language family and one of the twenty-two scheduled languages of the Republic of India. It is one of the six classical languages recognized by the Government of India and ranks as the 14th most spoken native language globally.

Language Context:

- **Modern Standard Telugu:** Based on the dialects of the Krishna, Guntur, East, and West Godavari districts of Coastal Andhra, Modern Standard Telugu is used in formal settings and literature.

Geographic Distribution:

- **States and Union Territories:** Telugu is primarily spoken in Andhra Pradesh and Telangana. It is also used in the Yanam district of Puducherry and spoken in parts of Karnataka, Tamil Nadu, Maharashtra, Chhattisgarh, Odisha, and West Bengal.
- **Diaspora:** The language is prevalent among the Telugu diaspora in the United States, Australia, Malaysia, Mauritius, UAE, Saudi Arabia, and other countries. Telugu is the fastest-growing Indian language in the US, especially in states like New Jersey and New York City.

Historical and Cultural Significance:

- **Historical Evolution:** Telugu split from Proto-Dravidian around 1000 BCE. Earliest inscriptions with Telugu words date back to approximately 400 BCE. The language was historically used by various South Indian dynasties and played a significant role in the administrative and cultural contexts.
- **Literary Tradition:** Telugu boasts a rich literary heritage spanning over a thousand years, with significant contributions to mathematics, literature, and arts. The tradition includes diverse genres and forms, with notable works like Pavuluri Mallana's Sāra Sangraha Ganitamu (11th century) and the cultivation of Avadhānaṃ, a complex literary performance.
- **Colonial and Post-Independence Period:** The influence of English began in the late 19th and early 20th centuries due to British rule. Since independence, Telugu has become widely used in media, education, and government. The Andhra Pradesh Official Language Act of 1966 established Telugu as the official language of Andhra Pradesh and Telangana.
- **Cultural Celebrations:** Telugu Language Day is celebrated on August 29, honoring the birthday of Telugu poet Gidugu

Venkata Ramamurthy. The World Telugu Conference, held every few years, addresses issues related to Telugu language policy and promotion.

Additional Official Language: English

- **English:** English, as part of Indian English (IE), is an official language in Andhra Pradesh and Telangana. It is used in government, legal, and educational contexts, and it serves as a critical bridge language in a multilingual nation.

Telugu is a vital language in Andhra Pradesh and Telangana, with significant historical, cultural, and administrative importance. It is supported by a robust literary tradition and has a growing global presence due to diaspora communities. English complements Telugu in official and educational settings, facilitating broader communication and governance.

Arunachal Pradesh:

Official Language: English

- **English:** English is the official language of Arunachal Pradesh. It is used for official and administrative purposes, as well as for communication within the government. English, along with Hindi, is a major language used by the Indian government, and it is the sole official language of the Indian Judiciary.

Language Context:

- **Indian English (IE):** Indian English is a group of English dialects spoken in India and among the Indian diaspora. It has evolved from British Indian English and has developed unique features influenced by local languages and cultural contexts. English is one of the 22 scheduled languages of India and plays a significant role in administration, education, and judiciary.

- **Regional Usage:** English is used extensively across India, including Arunachal Pradesh, for official documentation, education, and in the judiciary. The use of English ensures standardized communication across the diverse linguistic landscape of India.

Additional Information:

- **Arunachal Pradesh's Language Diversity:** Arunachal Pradesh is known for its linguistic diversity, with several indigenous languages spoken by various tribes in the state. These include languages such as Adi, Nyishi, Apatani, and Mishing, among others.
- **Importance of English:** The use of English in Arunachal Pradesh facilitates communication in government and educational institutions, and it helps bridge linguistic gaps within a multilingual state.

Geographic Distribution:

- **State Use:** In Arunachal Pradesh, English is the primary language of communication for official purposes. It is used in government offices, legal proceedings, and educational institutions.
- **Educational and Administrative Role:** English is used in schools and higher education institutions as a medium of instruction and is crucial for administrative functions and governance in the state.

English serves as the official language of Arunachal Pradesh, playing a central role in administration, legal proceedings, and education. It is a key language for communication across India's diverse linguistic landscape and is integral to the functioning of the state's government and educational systems.

Assam:

Official Language: Assamese

Assamese: Assamese, also known as Asamiya, is an Indo-Aryan language primarily spoken in the Indian state of Assam. It is the official language of Assam and serves as a lingua franca in the region. Assamese is spoken by over 15 million people and has a rich literary tradition. Historically, it was the court language of the Ahom kingdom from the 17th century.

Dialect Influence:

- **Nefamese**: An Assamese-based pidgin used in Arunachal Pradesh, replaced by Hindi.
- **Nagamese**: An Assamese-based Creole language used in Nagaland.
- **Kamtapuri**: A language closely related to Assamese, spoken in parts of Bangladesh and India.

Script and Writing: Assamese is written in the Assamese script, an abugida system. Historically, it has also been written using Latin and Eastern-Nagari scripts.

Historical Development:

- **Origins**: Assamese evolved from Middle Indo-Aryan Magadhi Prakrit before the 7th century CE.
- **Early Assamese**: Began to take shape in the 13th century with notable works such as Hema Sarasvati's "Prahrāda Carita" and Madhava Kandali's Assamese Ramayana.
- **Middle Assamese**: Saw the rise of Assamese as the court language during the Ahom kingdom and the development of standardized prose in Buranjis.
- **Modern Assamese**: Gained prominence with the advent of printing in the early 19th century. After initial setbacks, Assamese was reinstated as the official language of Assam in 1873.

Geographic Distribution: Assamese is native to Assam and spoken in parts of Arunachal Pradesh, Meghalaya, and Nagaland. It also has historical influence in Burma and Nepal.

Boro (Bodo):

- **Language Family**: Sino-Tibetan
- **Speakers**: Primarily spoken by the Boro people in Northeast India, Nepal, and Bangladesh.
- **Status**: Official language of Assam, taught up to the secondary level, and offered as a postgraduate course at the University of Guwahati.
- **Script**: Written in Devanagari script since 1975.

Additional Official Languages: Bengali

Bengali

- **Language Family**: Indo-Aryan
- **Speakers**: Approximately 234 million native speakers; also spoken by significant populations in India, Bangladesh, and the diaspora.
- **Status**: Official language of Bangladesh, West Bengal, Tripura, and Barak Valley in Assam; second official language in Jharkhand.
- **Historical Development**:
    - **Early**: Evolved from Magadhi Prakrit and Apabhraṃśa.
    - **Medieval**: Influenced by Arabic, Persian, and Turkic languages; saw development during the Bengal Sultanate.
    - **Modern**: Developed a standardized form during the 19th and early 20th centuries; highly influenced by Sanskrit, Persian, Arabic, and other languages.

Notable Movements: The Bengali Language Movement (1948-1956) led to the recognition of Bengali as a state language in Pakistan, and subsequently as a major factor in the creation of Bangladesh in

1971. International Mother Language Day is celebrated on February 21 to honour the Bengali language movement.

Modern Efforts: In 2022, the UN adopted Bangla as an unofficial language following a resolution by India, and there have been proposals to make Bengali an official UN language.

Bihar:

Official Language: Hindi

Modern Standard Hindi, commonly referred to as Hindi, is an Indo-Aryan language predominantly spoken in North India. It serves as the lingua franca of the Hindi Belt region, which includes parts of northern, central, eastern, and western India.

Script: Hindi is written in the Devanagari script, an abugida consisting of 11 vowels and 33 consonants, written from left to right.

Status:

- **Official Language:** Hindi is one of the two official languages of the Government of India, alongside English.
- **Regional Official Language:** It is the official language in nine Indian states and three union territories and acts as an additional official language in three other states.
- **Scheduled Language:** It is one of the 22 scheduled languages recognized by the Republic of India.

Linguistic Classification:

- **Hindustani:** Hindi is a standardized and Sanskrit zed register of Hindustani, which is based primarily on the Khariboli dialect of Delhi and the surrounding areas.
- **Mutual Intelligibility:** Standard Hindi is mutually intelligible with Standard Urdu, another register of Hindustani, due to their shared colloquial base.

Historical Background

Origins:

- **Sanskrit Roots:** Hindi is a direct descendant of early forms of Vedic Sanskrit, transitioning through Shauraseni Prakrit and Śauraseni Apabhraṃśa. This evolution took place from the 7th century CE onwards.

Development:

- **From Apabhraṃśa to Hindi:** Over time, Shauraseni Apabhraṃśa, a form of Prakrit, evolved into the medieval forms of Hindi, enriched by influences from Persian and Arabic during the Delhi Sultanate and Mughal periods.
- **Modern Standardization:** In the 19th century, Hindi underwent standardization and Sanskritization, leading to the form known today as Modern Standard Hindi.

Etymology and Terminology:

Historical Terms:

- **Hindī:** The term originally referred to the inhabitants of the Indo-Gangetic Plain and was borrowed from Classical Persian Hindī (Iranian Persian pronunciation: Hendi), meaning "of or belonging to Hind (India)."
- **Hindavī/Hinduī:** These terms were used historically to denote the language of the Indian people, as seen in poetry by Amir Khusrau.

Linguistic Evolution:

- **Sindhu to Hindi:** The terms "Hindi" and "Hindu" derive from the Old Persian term Sindhu (सिन्धु), referring to the Indus River. The Greek terms "Indus" and "India" are cognates referring to the river and the land, respectively.

Geographic and Demographic Reach:

Global Presence:

- **Most-Spoken Language:** Hindi is the fourth most-spoken first language globally, after Mandarin, Spanish, and English. Including Urdu (a mutually intelligible language), it ranks as the third most-spoken language worldwide.
- **Growth:** Hindi is the fastest-growing language in India, with significant increases in speakers compared to other languages.

Regional Varieties:

- **Bazaar Hindustani:** Simplified or pidginized forms of Hindi used in regions where Hindi is not the primary language.
- **Haflong Hindi:** A pidginized variety spoken in Haflong, Assam, among speakers of other native languages.

This overview captures the essence of Modern Standard Hindi, its historical development, and its role both within India and internationally.

Hindustani and its Evolution:

Hindustani: During the Delhi Sultanate period (roughly from the 12th to 16th centuries), which covered much of what is now northern India, eastern Pakistan, southern Nepal, and Bangladesh, the interaction between Hindu and Muslim cultures led to significant linguistic changes. The Sanskrit and Prakrit base of Old Hindi was enriched with Persian loanwords, evolving into the language known as Hindustani. This process resulted in the development of a vernacular language that was a blend of these diverse influences.

Role and Influence:

- **Expression of Unity:** Hindustani became a symbol of Indian national unity during the Indian Independence movement. Its widespread use across various regions and communities helped foster a sense of common identity.

- **Cultural Impact:** The language is prominently featured in Bollywood films and songs, reflecting its continued influence and importance in Indian culture.

Standard Hindi:

- **Basis and Evolution:** Modern Standard Hindi is based on the Delhi dialect, which emerged as the prestige dialect, replacing earlier literary languages such as Awadhi and Braj. This form of Hindi resulted from the assimilation of Persian and Arabic vocabulary into the Khariboli dialect.
- **Literary Examples:** Early examples of Standard Hindi literature include:
  - *Prēm Sāgar* by Lallu Lal
  - *Batiyāl Pachīsī* by Sadal Misra
  - *Rānī Kētakī Kī Kahānī* by Insha Allah Khan These works were published in the Devanagari script during the early 19th century.

Official Status of Hindi:

- **In India:** Hindi is an official language in the following states: Bihar, Chhattisgarh, Haryana, Himachal Pradesh, Jharkhand, Madhya Pradesh, Rajasthan, Uttar Pradesh, and Uttarakhand. It is also an official language in Gujarat (alongside Gujarati) and an additional official language in West Bengal (in regions where over 10% of the population speaks Hindi). Hindi holds official status in the Union Territories of Delhi, Andaman and Nicobar Islands, and Dadra and Nagar Haveli and Daman and Diu.

Hindi Outside India:

- **Fiji:** In Fiji, an Awadhi dialect with influences from Bhojpuri, Bihari languages, Fijian, and English is spoken. Known as "Fiji Hindi," it has been recognized as an official language under the 1997 Constitution of Fiji. The 2013 Constitution continued to recognize it as "Fiji Hindi." It is spoken by approximately 380,000 people in Fiji.

- **Nepal:** In Nepal, Hindi is spoken by around 77,569 people as a first language and by 1,225,950 people as a second language according to the 2011 Nepal census. A notable incident occurred in 2008 when Indian-born Paramananda Jha, elected as vice-president of Nepal, took his oath in Hindi, leading to significant controversy and protests. The Nepal Supreme Court later ruled the oath in Hindi as invalid.
- **South Africa:** Hindi is a protected language under the South African Constitution. The Pan South African Language Board is tasked with promoting and ensuring respect for Hindi, along with other languages. Despite the presence of Hindi and other Indian languages in South Africa for over 125 years, there has been limited academic study of these languages' usage, evolution, and current status.
- **United Arab Emirates:** Hindi has been adopted as the third official court language in the Emirate of Abu Dhabi. This status allows the Indian workforce in the UAE to file complaints to labor courts in their native language.

This overview captures the evolution of Hindustani into Modern Standard Hindi, its official status in various regions, and its presence and influence beyond India.

Geographic Distribution of Hindi:

1. India:

- **Northern India:** Hindi is the primary language and serves as the lingua franca in northern India, encompassing the Hindi Belt. This region includes states like Uttar Pradesh, Madhya Pradesh, Rajasthan, Haryana, and parts of Bihar, Jharkhand, and Uttarakhand.
- **Northeast India:**
    - **Haflong Hindi:** In Haflong, Assam, a pidgin known as Haflong Hindi has developed as a lingua franca among speakers of various native languages.

- **Arunachal Pradesh:** Hindi serves as a lingua franca among the diverse population that speaks over 50 different dialects.

2. **Pakistan:**
   - **Mutual Intelligibility:** Hindi is easily understood by many Pakistanis, particularly those who speak Urdu. Both languages are standard registers of Hindustani and share a common colloquial base. Additionally, Indian media, including films and television, are widely viewed in Pakistan.

3. **Afghanistan:**
   - **Kabul and Surroundings:** A significant number of people in Kabul and other areas can speak and understand Hindi-Urdu, largely due to the influence of Bollywood films, songs, and actors.

4. **Nepal:**
   - **Madheshis:** Hindi is spoken by a substantial number of Madheshis, people with roots in northern India who migrated to Nepal over centuries. According to the 2011 Nepal census, Hindi is spoken by about 8 million people in Nepal, including both first and second-language speakers.

5. **Indian Diaspora:**
   - **United States:** Approximately 863,077 Hindi speakers.
   - **United Kingdom:** Around 45,800 Hindi speakers.
   - **United Arab Emirates:** Significant Hindi-speaking community, particularly among the Indian workforce.
   - **Trinidad and Tobago:** About 26,000 Hindi speakers.
   - **Guyana:** Significant Hindi-speaking population.
   - **Suriname:** Approximately 150,000 Hindi speakers.
   - **South Africa:** About 250,292 Hindi speakers.
   - **Fiji:** Approximately 380,000 speakers of Fiji Hindi.
   - **Mauritius:** Around 450,170 Hindi speakers.

- **Uganda:** About 100,000 Hindi speakers.
- **New Zealand:** Around 20,000 Hindi speakers.
- **Germany:** Approximately 20,000 Hindi speakers.
- **Singapore:** About 3,000 Hindi speakers.

Hindi's geographic distribution highlights its significant presence not only in northern India but also among the Indian diaspora across various continents. Its influence extends into neighbouring countries and regions, reflecting its status as a major global language.

Comparison Between Hindi and Urdu:

Linguistic Similarities and Differences:

- **Mutual Intelligibility:** Hindi and Urdu are two standardized registers of the same language, known collectively as Hindustani or Hindi-Urdu. They share a core vocabulary derived from native Prakrit and Sanskrit roots, and their grammar is identical. This makes them mutually intelligible.
- **Vocabulary and Etymology:**
    - **Hindi:** Has a larger proportion of Sanskrit-derived words. It uses the Devanagari script and tends to include more tatsam (directly borrowed from Sanskrit) words.
    - **Urdu:** Uses more Arabic and Persian loanwords and is written in the Perso-Arabic script. It tends to include more tadbhav (evolved from Sanskrit) and videshi (foreign) words.

Script:

- **Hindi:** Written in Devanagari script, which is an abugida. This script consists of 11 vowels and 33 consonants and is written from left to right. While Devanagari is not entirely phonetic for Hindi, it has distinct phonological rules compared to Sanskrit.

- **Urdu:** Written in the Perso-Arabic script, which is written from right to left and is an alphabetic script. This script has a different set of letters and phonetic representations compared to Devanagari.

Etymology and Vocabulary Categories:

1. **Tatsam:** Words directly borrowed from Sanskrit without modification. E.g., Hindi "नाम" (nāma) and Sanskrit "नाम" (nāma), both meaning "name."
2. **Ardhatatsam:** Words borrowed from Sanskrit that have undergone phonological changes. E.g., Hindi "सूरज" (sūraj) from Sanskrit "सूर्य" (sūrya).
3. **Tadbhav:** Native words in Hindi evolved from Sanskrit through phonological changes. E.g., Sanskrit "कर्म" (karma) becomes Hindi "काम" (kām).
4. **Deshaj:** Words not derived from Indo-Aryan languages, including onomatopoetic words and borrowings from non-Indo-Aryan languages.
5. **Videshi:** Loanwords from non-Indo-Aryan languages, like Persian, Arabic, English, and Portuguese. E.g., Hindi "क़िला" (qila) from Persian.

Influence and Sanskritization:

- **Sanskrit Influence:** Hindi has a significant amount of vocabulary borrowed from Sanskrit, especially in formal and academic contexts. The formal variant known as Śuddh Hindi aims to use more Sanskrit-derived terms and is considered prestigious.
- **Persian Influence:** Hindi features many Persian loanwords due to historical influence under the Delhi Sultanate and Mughal Empire. Persian borrowings peaked in the 17th century but have since decreased with the Sanskritization of Hindi. Some Persian words are still widely used in

Standard Hindi and Urdu poetry.

6. **Arabic Influence:** Many Persian loanwords in Hindi were originally borrowed from Arabic. Examples include "मुस्कलि" (muśkil, "difficult") and "कताब" (kitāb, "book").

Cultural and Political Status:

- **Hindi:** One of the two official languages of India, alongside English. It is the most commonly used scheduled language in India and serves as a lingua franca in the Hindi Belt. Hindi has official status in several states and union territories.
- **Urdu:** The national language and lingua franca of Pakistan. In India, Urdu is one of the 22 scheduled languages and holds official status in several states and union territories. It is also used in literary and cultural contexts, particularly in poetry.

Hindi and Urdu are two registers of the same language, sharing a core vocabulary and grammar while differing in script and vocabulary sources. Hindi is influenced more by Sanskrit, while Urdu incorporates more Persian and Arabic elements. Both languages have played significant roles in their respective regions and continue to influence each other's development and usage.

Additional Official Language: Urdu

Hindi:

- An Indo-Aryan language primarily spoken in India.
- Official language of the Indian Union alongside English.
- Written in Devanagari script.
- Utilizes a significant amount of Sanskrit-derived vocabulary.
- Standardized forms include Modern Standard Hindi and regional varieties.

Urdu:

- An Indo-Aryan language spoken mainly in Pakistan and parts of India.
- National language and lingua franca of Pakistan; also has official status in several Indian states.
- Written in the Perso-Arabic script.
- Incorporates a considerable amount of Persian and Arabic vocabulary.
- Standardized forms include those of Delhi, Lucknow, and Karachi.

Linguistic Similarities and Differences:

Similarities:

- **Vocabulary:** Both Hindi and Urdu share a core vocabulary derived from native Prakrit and Sanskrit roots.
- **Grammar:** The grammatical structure of Hindi and Urdu is nearly identical.
- **Phonology:** Both languages share similar phonological systems.

Differences:

- **Script:** Hindi uses the Devanagari script, while Urdu uses the Perso-Arabic script.
- **Vocabulary Influence:** Hindi incorporates more Sanskrit-derived words, while Urdu features more Arabic and Persian loanwords.
- **Formality:** Urdu and Hindi are mutually intelligible in colloquial speech, but their mutual intelligibility decreases in formal contexts due to differing literary and technical vocabularies.

Historical Context:

Hindi:

- Evolved from Shauraseni Prakrit.
- Influenced by Sanskrit, particularly in its formal and technical vocabulary.
- Underwent Sanskritization in the 19th century, which aimed to replace Persian and Arabic vocabulary with Sanskrit-derived terms.

Urdu:

- Developed from the Apabhraṃśa register of Shauraseni and became a Persianized form of Hindustani.
- Emerged as a literary language in the 18th century and was significantly influenced by Persian, especially during the Mughal Empire.
- The name "Urdu" was introduced around 1780 and means "army" in Turkic, reflecting its historical role as a lingua franca among military camps.

Colonial and Post-Colonial Periods:

Colonial India:

- Urdu replaced Persian as the official language of northern India in 1837.
- British policies promoted Urdu in Muslim-majority regions, while Hindi was used by Hindus, leading to a linguistic and cultural divide.
- The Hindi–Urdu controversy emerged, leading to the formal distinction between the languages, particularly with the partition of India in 1947.

Post-Partition:

- **India:** Urdu remains significant in cultural contexts but faces challenges due to the dominance of Hindi and socio-economic factors.
- **Pakistan:** Urdu was promoted as a unifying national language but faces competition from regional languages and English. Attempts at Urduization have been partially successful.

Demographics and Geographic Distribution:

India:

- Urdu is spoken widely in areas with significant Muslim populations and historical Muslim influence.
- There are over 100 million native speakers in India, with Urdu being prominent in states like Uttar Pradesh, Bihar, and Telangana.

Pakistan:

- Urdu is the lingua franca and serves as the primary language of communication among diverse ethnic groups.
- It is taught in schools and used in media, but it is not the native language of most Pakistanis. The majority of native speakers are Muhajirs (Muslim migrants from India).

Cultural and Linguistic Identity:

India:

- Urdu is associated with Muslim cultural heritage and has a significant presence in Indian media and literature. However, the number of speakers has declined in recent years due to socio-economic and political factors.

Pakistan:

- Urdu symbolizes national unity and cultural identity. It is used in education and media but competes with regional languages and English.

Challenges and Future:

Hindi:

- Faces challenges due to the dominance of English and the need for modernization in certain vocabulary areas. Efforts to maintain the language include Sanskritization and promoting its use in various domains.

Urdu:

- Faces challenges related to its script, socio-economic status, and competition with other languages. The debate over the use of Devanagari or Roman scripts for Urdu continues, and efforts to preserve and promote the language are ongoing.

This comparison highlights the linguistic, historical, and cultural contexts of both languages, reflecting their shared origins and distinct paths of development.

Chhattisgarh:

Official Language: Hindi

Additional Official Language: Chhattisgarhi

Chhattisgarhi is indeed an Indo-Aryan language spoken primarily in the Indian state of Chhattisgarh and also in parts of Odisha, Madhya Pradesh, and Maharashtra. Here are some key points about Chhattisgarhi:

Overview:

- **Speakers:** Approximately 16.25 million.
- **Official Status:** Official language of the state of Chhattisgarh.
- **Language Family:** Indo-Aryan, within the Eastern Hindi languages group.

Linguistic Classification:

- **Dialects:** Chhattisgarhi is often classified as a dialect of Hindi in the Indian national census. However, it has distinct linguistic features that set it apart from Standard Hindi.
- **Related Languages:** It shares linguistic similarities with other Eastern Hindi languages and dialects, such as Bagheli and Awadhi.

Linguistic Features:

- **Phonology:** Chhattisgarhi features a phonological system that includes sounds and pronunciation patterns distinct from Standard Hindi.
- **Grammar:** It retains many features of the dialects from which it evolved, including variations in verb conjugation, pronouns, and sentence structure.
- **Vocabulary:** Chhattisgarhi vocabulary includes elements unique to the region, along with shared vocabulary with Hindi.

Cultural and Regional Importance:

- **Literature and Media:** Chhattisgarhi has a rich tradition of folk literature, music, and oral storytelling. Modern Chhattisgarhi literature and media have grown, contributing to the cultural identity of the region.
- **Cultural Identity:** The language is a key part of the cultural identity of people in Chhattisgarh and surrounding regions. It reflects the history and traditions of the area.

Recognition and Development:

- **Official Language:** In Chhattisgarh, Chhattisgarhi is used in official documents, education, and local government. Its status as the official language supports its use in various domains of public life.
- **Education:** Efforts are made to promote Chhattisgarhi in schools and educational institutions within the state. There are also initiatives to preserve and develop the language.

Chhattisgarhi's classification as a dialect of Hindi may reflect its close relationship with Hindi, but its unique characteristics and cultural significance highlight its distinct identity.

Konkani is an Indo-Aryan language spoken predominantly along the western coast of India. Here's a detailed overview of its geographical distribution and demographics:

Goa:

Official Language: Hindi

Geographical Distribution:

A. **Konkan Division of Maharashtra:** The native region of Konkani speakers in Maharashtra includes the Konkan division, which stretches along the western coast of the state.

B. **Goa:** Goa is a major Konkani-speaking region. The language has a rich cultural presence here, and Goa is known for its vibrant Konkani literature and media.

C. **Daman:** The territory of Daman, part of the Daman and Diu Union Territory, also has a Konkani-speaking population.

D. **Karnataka:** In Karnataka, Konkani is spoken in the districts of Uttara Kannada, Udupi, Dakshina Kannada, Belagavi, Mysore, and Bengaluru. Each district has its own dialects and variations of the language.

E. **Kerala:** Konkani is spoken in districts such as Kasaragod, Kochi, Alappuzha, Thiruvananthapuram, and Kottayam in Kerala. The language in Kerala exhibits significant regional influences.

Dialects and Variations:

- **Dialectal Diversity:** Konkani exhibits a variety of dialects, each with distinct pronunciation, vocabulary, tone, and sometimes, grammar. These variations reflect the historical and regional influences on the language.

Demographic Statistics:

- **2001 Census:** Approximately 2,489,016 Konkani speakers in India.
- **2011 Census:** The number of Konkani speakers was recorded as 2,256,502, accounting for 0.19% of India's population.
    - **Distribution:**
        - Karnataka: 788,294
        - Goa: 964,305
        - Maharashtra: 399,255
        - Kerala: 69,449
- **Growth Rate:** Konkani experienced a 9.34% decrease in the number of speakers from 2001 to 2011. It is one of the few scheduled languages to have a negative growth rate during this period.

Diaspora and Migration:

- **Historical Migration:** During Portuguese rule in Goa and British colonial rule in India, many Konkani-speaking people migrated to various parts of the world, including Portuguese and British colonies and the pre-partition region of Pakistan.
- **Post-Colonial Migration:** The migratory trend continued into the post-colonial era, leading to significant Konkani-

speaking communities in countries such as Kenya, Uganda, Pakistan, the Persian Gulf countries, Portugal, the European Union, the British Isles, and other parts of the Anglosphere.
- **Language Influence:** In the diaspora, Konkani dialects have been influenced by the languages of the host countries, leading to variations in how Konkani is spoken abroad.

Challenges and Preservation:

- **Minority Language:** Konkani is often not recognized by censuses and surveys conducted in various countries where Konkani-speaking expatriates live, making it difficult to accurately determine the number of Konkani speakers globally.
- **Cultural Impact:** Despite migration and diaspora challenges, many Konkani families continue to speak their ancestral dialects, preserving their linguistic and cultural heritage.

Konkani's rich history and diverse regional presence highlight its importance in the cultural and linguistic landscape of western India and the broader global diaspora.

Gujarat:

Official Languages: Hindi

Gujarati:

- **Language Family & Origin**: Gujarati is an Indo-Aryan language that originated from Old Gujarati (c. 1100–1500 CE).
- **Official Status**:
    - One of India's 22 scheduled languages.
    - Official language of Gujarat state and the union territory of Dadra and Nagar Haveli and Daman and Diu.

- Speaker Population:
  - As of 2011, spoken by 55.5 million people (4.5% of India's population).
  - Ranked as the 6th most spoken language in India and 26th worldwide by native speakers (2007 data).
- **Growth:** The 2011 census places Gujarati as the third fastest-growing language in India, following Hindi and Kashmiri.
- **Diaspora & Global Presence:**
  - Widely spoken by Gujarati communities in Mumbai, Pakistan (especially Karachi), and by the Gujarati diaspora in the U.S., Canada, the UK, Southeast Africa (Kenya, Tanzania, Uganda, Zambia, South Africa), as well as Hong Kong, Singapore, Australia, and the Middle East.
  - In London, Gujarati is the 4th most spoken language.
- **Historical Stages:**
  - **Old Gujarati** (1200–1500 CE): Used by Gurjars; shares features with Rajasthani.
  - **Middle Gujarati** (1300–1800): Diverged from Rajasthani, developing distinct phonemes and grammar.
  - **Modern Gujarati**: Underwent phonological changes, with efforts to standardize it in the 1920s.
- **Significant Figures:** Mahatma Gandhi promoted Gujarati as a medium for literary expression and helped standardize its spelling in 1936.
- **Demographics (2022):**
  - About 62 million speakers globally, with major populations in India, Tanzania, Kenya, and Pakistan.
  - In the UK, over 200,000 speakers, largely in London and cities with East African Gujarati communities.
- **Education:**
  - Taught as a minority language in Rajasthan, Madhya Pradesh, Maharashtra, Tamil Nadu, Delhi, and offered

as a GCSE subject in the UK.

- **Language Maintenance:**
  - Gujarati parents in the diaspora are particularly inclined to pass on the language to their children, compared to other Indian language communities.
- **Diverse Speakers:** In Gujarat, many non-Gujaratis, such as the Kutchis, Parsis, and Hindu Sindhi refugees, also speak Gujarati.

Haryana:

Official Language: Hindi

Additional Official Language: English

Punjabi:

- **Language Family & Origin:** Punjabi is an Indo-Aryan language originating from Prakrit and Apabhraṃśa, with development beginning in the 7th century. It stabilized by the 10th century and became known as Old Punjabi, transitioning into Mediaeval Punjabi (16th–19th century).
- **Global Speaker Population:**
  - Approximately 113 million native speakers worldwide.
  - Most spoken language in Pakistan (80.5 million, 2017 census).
  - 11th most spoken language in India (31.1 million, 2011 census).
  - Widely spoken in Canada, the UK, the U.S., Australia, and the Gulf states.
- **Scripts:**
  - **Pakistan**: Written in Shahmukhi (Perso-Arabic script).
  - **India**: Written in Gurmukhi (Indic script).
- **Etymology:** Derived from Persian "Panj-āb" (Five Waters), referencing the Indus River and its five major tributaries in

the Punjab region.

- **Distinctive Linguistic Features**: Known for its use of lexical tone, uncommon among Indo-Aryan and Indo-European languages.
- **Cultural Influence**:
    - ♦ Significant Arabic and Persian vocabulary due to historical Muslim conquests.
    - ♦ Additional minor influences from Portuguese, Greek, Chagatai, Japanese, Chinese, and English.
- **Modern Punjabi Varieties**:
    - ♦ **Standard Punjabi (Majhi dialect)**: Predominantly spoken in the Amritsar-Lahore region and widely used in education and media.
    - ♦ **Eastern Punjabi**: Includes dialects like Malwai, Doabi, and Puadhi, spoken in Indian Punjab.
    - ♦ **Western Punjabi (Lahnda)**: Includes dialects like Saraiki, Pahari-Pothwari, and Hindko, spoken in Pakistan's Punjab region.
- **Official Status**:
    - ♦ **Pakistan**: Most widely spoken native language.
    - ♦ **India**: Official language of Punjab state and an additional official language in Haryana and Delhi.
- **Punjabi Diaspora**:
    - ♦ Major populations in Canada (670,000 in 2021), the UK (300,000 in 2011), and the U.S. (280,000).
    - ♦ Minority communities in Australia, Gulf states, and other regions.
- **Standardization:**
    - ♦ The Majhi dialect is the standard for media in both India and Pakistan.
    - ♦ The Gurmukhi script was developed by the Sikh Gurus based on Standard Punjabi.

Himachal Pradesh:

Official Language: Hindi

Additional Official Language: Sanskrit

Sanskrit:

- **Language Family & Origins**: Sanskrit belongs to the Indo-Aryan branch of Indo-European languages. It arose in South Asia, brought by Indo-Aryan tribes in the late Bronze Age, and is one of the three oldest documented languages in the Indo-European family.
- **Religious & Cultural Importance**: It is the sacred language of Hinduism and classical texts in Buddhism and Jainism. In ancient and medieval South Asia, and with the spread of Hindu and Buddhist traditions, Sanskrit influenced Southeast, East, and Central Asia as a language of high culture and political elite.
- Development & Varieties:
    - **Vedic Sanskrit** (1500–1200 BCE): Found in the Rigveda, it was heavily influenced by indigenous languages, especially Dravidian. The Rigveda's preservation aids in reconstructing Proto-Indo-European.
    - **Classical Sanskrit**: Codified by Pāṇini's *Aṣṭādhyāyī* in the mid-1st millennium BCE. Used by dramatists like Kālidāsa and in foundational mathematical texts.
    - **Epic Sanskrit**: The language of *Mahābhārata* and *Rāmāyaṇa*, oral epics spanning 400 BCE–300 CE.
- **Script & Writing**: Sanskrit has been transcribed in various Brahmic scripts since around the 1st millennium CE, now commonly written in Devanagari.
- **Etymology:** The term "Sanskrit" means "well-formed" or "perfected" (from *sáṃskṛta*). Sound was central to its sacred nature, viewed as a fundamental representation of creation and liberation.

- **Relation to Prakrits**: Competing with vernacular Prakritic languages, Sanskrit was seen as grammatically refined, whereas Prakrit was regarded as "natural" and instinctive.
- **Historical Texts & Influence**:
  - The *Ṛg-veda*, a primary text of Vedic Sanskrit, exhibits linguistic stability, suggesting a set linguistic form by the late 2nd millennium BCE.
  - Other significant texts include the *Sāmaveda*, *Yajurveda*, *Atharvaveda*, and Upanishads, showcasing regional dialects.
  - The language spread beyond India, evidenced in treaties and inscriptions like the Mitanni Treaty, containing early Vedic terms and deities.
- **Modern Status**: Included in India's Eighth Schedule languages, Sanskrit has minimal native speakers but remains a ceremonial language in Hindu and Buddhist rituals. Educational institutions like the Benares Sanskrit College (founded 1791) continue its legacy.
- **Influence on Other Languages**: Sanskrit profoundly impacted the lexicon and structure of South, Southeast, and East Asian languages, particularly in learned and formal vocabularies.

This comprehensive overview of Sanskrit's evolution and influence highlights its remarkable journey from a sacred, early Vedic language to the refined Classical Sanskrit. This language standardization, largely driven by Pāṇini's *Aṣṭādhyāyī*, helped establish Sanskrit as the principal scholarly and literary language across India and beyond for over two millennia. Here are some of the key points from this history:

A. **Development of Classical Sanskrit**: Early Vedic Sanskrit was distinct, evolving into Classical Sanskrit around the mid-1st millennium BCE, marked significantly by Pāṇini's grammatical codification. The *Aṣṭādhyāyī* synthesized previous grammatical efforts and set a linguistic standard upheld in scholarly works and debates, including those observed by the Chinese pilgrim Xuanzang.

B. **Linguistic Rigor and Flexibility**: Pāṇini's work enabled a balanced language—both controlled for grammatical accuracy and flexible enough to accommodate evolving literary demands. With refined syntax and a robust vocabulary, Classical Sanskrit facilitated philosophical discourse, religious texts, and literary creativity across genres and eras.

C. **Sanskrit vs. Prakrit Languages**: Sanskrit coexisted with Prakrit languages, like Pali and Ardhamagadhi, often preferred by Buddhist and Jain thinkers. While Prakrits became vernacular dialects accessible to commoners, Sanskrit was maintained by the learned elite. The dynamic between Sanskrit and Prakrits resembles Latin and vernacular languages in medieval Europe.

D. **Sanskrit as a Pan-Asian Language of Culture**: Sanskrit's precision and formal structure helped it transcend linguistic borders, making it an essential medium for Hindu and Buddhist teachings throughout Asia. From China to Southeast Asia, Sanskrit texts enriched intellectual and spiritual traditions, promoted by scholars and pilgrims like Faxian and Xuanzang.

E. **Dravidian Influence**: Dravidian languages, particularly Tamil, impacted Sanskrit's phonology, syntax, and vocabulary. Features like retroflex sounds and verb forms in Classical Sanskrit may stem from early interactions between Indo-Aryan and Dravidian communities, suggesting a deep linguistic and cultural exchange.

F. **Enduring Legacy and Cultural Impact**: Sanskrit became a cultural glue across India, allowing for shared intellectual pursuits and ritual practices. It functioned as a learned lingua franca, connecting scholars and serving as a conduit for religious and philosophical ideas that shaped regional cultures and languages.

Today, while its spoken use is limited, Sanskrit remains foundational in many Indian languages and cultural practices, representing a historical thread that unites diverse linguistic communities across the subcontinent. Its rigorous grammar and intellectual richness continue to inspire linguists, historians, and philosophers alike.

Decline: The decline of Sanskrit began around the 13th century, aligning with the onset of Islamic invasions in South Asia, which eventually established Muslim rule through various Sultanates and the Mughal Empire. Sheldon Pollock attributes this decline to a shift in "cultural, social, and political" dynamics rather than the "struggle with barbarous invaders," suggesting that the vernacular languages became more appealing for literary works. As major centers of Sanskrit literature, like Kashmir, fell, Sanskrit creativity diminished, with Kashmir's literary activity extinguished possibly due to repeated conflicts, including the Mongol invasion of 1320.

With Hindu kingdoms in southern and eastern India, such as the Vijayanagara Empire, Sanskrit's influence also waned. Nonetheless, there were periods where Sanskrit was patronized, such as during Emperor Akbar's reign. The spread of Persian by Muslim rulers encouraged linguistic adaptation among Indians for governmental roles, while Hindu leaders like Shivaji later sought to revive Sanskrit.

Although Pollock contends that Sanskrit experienced a form of death after the 12th century, as innovation in its literature reduced mainly to hymn-writing, other scholars argue that it simply declined. Jurgen Hanneder, for instance, critiques Pollock's hypothesis, suggesting the absence of creative literature does not necessarily prove Sanskrit's death. Moriz Winternitz and Brian Hatcher similarly assert that Sanskrit remained integral in Hindu rituals, drama, and festivals, though less prevalent than in earlier centuries.

Sanskrit's influence on modern Indo-Aryan languages, such as Hindi and Bengali, is deeply rooted. Colin Masica explains that Old Indo-Aryan (1500 BCE–600 BCE) encompasses Vedic Sanskrit, while Middle Indo-Aryan (600 BCE–1000 CE) includes Prakrit languages like Pali, which contributed to the foundation of modern languages.

Modern Indo-Aryan languages likely evolved from Sanskrit mixed with regional dialects, producing diverse linguistic traditions across India.

Geographic Distribution of Sanskrit:

- **Widespread Historical Presence**: Sanskrit was historically present beyond South Asia, reaching Southeast Asia and Central Asia through monks, religious pilgrims, and merchants as early as the 1st millennium CE.
- **Collections and Manuscripts**: South Asia holds the largest collection of ancient Sanskrit manuscripts. Additionally, significant Sanskrit texts have been found in China, Myanmar, Indonesia, and Tibet.
- **Broader Reach**: Sanskrit inscriptions have also been discovered in regions like Afghanistan, Nepal, Mongolia, Uzbekistan, Tajikistan, Korea, and Japan.

Official Status of Sanskrit:

- **India's Official Language**: Sanskrit is one of the 22 official languages in India. In 2010, Uttarakhand declared it a second official language, followed by Himachal Pradesh in 2019.

Scripts for Sanskrit:

A. **Brahmi Script**:
   - Developed as a modified consonant-syllabic script that includes ligatures and diacritics.
   - Evolved into numerous forms, adaptable to virtually any Brahmi-based script.

B. **Nagari Script**:
   - Dates back to the 1st millennium CE, fully developing into Devanagari and Nandinagari by the end of the first millennium.
   - Became prominent for Sanskrit from the 18th century and has a large repertoire of characters and phonetic accuracy markers like the visarga and anusvara.

C. **Other Scripts**:

- ♦ Regional scripts like Gujarati, Bangla-Assamese, and south Indian scripts (Kannada, Telugu, Malayalam, Grantha) have also been used for Sanskrit.
- ♦ Despite visual differences, these scripts share similar phonetic systems based on the Brahmi structure.

Transliteration and Romanization:

- **IAST Standard**: The International Alphabet of Sanskrit Transliteration (IAST) has been widely used since the 19th century, with ASCII-based schemes (e.g., ITRANS) for digital compatibility.
- **Western Usage**: Romanized transliteration became common in Western academic texts in the 20th century for ease of reproduction.

Sanskrit Epigraphy:

- **Earliest Inscriptions**: Stone inscriptions in Brahmi script date back to the 1st century BCE, including significant inscriptions in Mathura from the 1st and 2nd centuries CE.
- **Regional Spread**: By the 4th century, Sanskrit became the dominant language for inscriptions across the Indian subcontinent and extended to South and Southeast Asia, recorded on various materials (stone, metal, terracotta).
- **Southeast Asian Influence**: Early Sanskrit inscriptions appear by the 5th century CE in countries like Vietnam, Malaysia, and Indonesia, often using South Indian Pallava script influences that later evolved into regional scripts.
- The literature and influence of Sanskrit extend across numerous genres and regions, showcasing its lasting cultural and linguistic impact.

Literature in Sanskrit:

- Sanskrit literature is divided into Vedic and Classical Sanskrit periods. Vedic Sanskrit primarily comprises religious and liturgical works, including the four Vedas, Brāhmaṇas, and Sūtras. Conversely, Classical Sanskrit literature spans diverse subjects like epics, drama, romance, law, politics, philosophy, medicine, and astronomy. While Vedic literature exudes optimism, portraying human capability and fulfillment, later literature becomes more introspective and fate-oriented, reflecting philosophical developments around karma and reincarnation.

Influence on Indian Languages:

- For over two millennia, Sanskrit influenced the Indian subcontinent's languages, with many modern Indo-Aryan, Dravidian, and Munda languages adopting Sanskrit vocabulary and grammatical structures. For instance, Hindi evolved as a Sanskritized form of Hindustani. Similarly, Marathi, Telugu, and Kannada reflect extensive Sanskrit influence, with borrowed terms (tatsama) and modified forms (tadbhava). The Dravidian languages—especially Kannada, Telugu, Malayalam, and Tamil—integrated Sanskrit elements into their vocabulary, morphology, and phonetics, showing the adaptability of Sanskrit within diverse linguistic systems.

Influence Beyond India:

- Sanskrit reached Southeast Asia, Central Asia, and East Asia along with Buddhism, impacting local languages, primarily through religious vocabulary. Buddhist Sanskrit influenced Sino-Tibetan languages like Chinese, where transliterations of Sanskrit terms began as early as 200 CE. Chinese monks transliterated and translated Sanskrit texts, impacting vocabulary across East Asia. In Japan, Sanskrit continues to hold religious significance in the Shingon sect of esoteric Buddhism, preserving transliterations of Sanskrit terms and mantras.
- Sanskrit's linguistic heritage spans not only as a formal language of religious, scholarly, and royal discourse but

also as a profound influence on vocabulary, grammar, and linguistic structure in languages across South and East Asia. Its adaptability and linguistic richness contributed to its survival and influence for centuries, making it an enduring cultural foundation in the region.

- Sanskrit's influence stretches well beyond South Asia, permeating Southeast Asia and even reaching the West through vocabulary related to food and other fields.

Influence in Southeast Asia:

- Sanskrit inscriptions across Southeast Asia reflect its historical influence in the region, with many languages adopting Sanskrit vocabulary. For example, Indonesian, Thai, Lao, and Khmer languages contain numerous Sanskrit loanwords, with languages like Javanese borrowing nearly half of its older vocabulary from Sanskrit. Similarly, Malay, evolving into modern Malaysian and Indonesian, and even Philippine languages like Tagalog, contain traces of Sanskrit influence, albeit with fewer Sanskrit roots than in other regional languages.
- In Southeast Asia, the term *bhāṣā* (meaning "spoken language" in Sanskrit) is widely used in naming languages, reflecting cultural and linguistic ties to Sanskrit traditions. Even today, Thai and other Southeast Asian languages continue to draw upon Sanskrit for technical and specialized vocabulary.

Influence in Indonesia:

- Indonesia showcases a particularly deep-rooted Sanskrit influence, with its earliest Sanskrit text found in East Borneo dating back to 400 CE. Indianization introduced Sanskrit as a cultural rather than religious influence, leading to the widespread adoption of Sanskrit words and concepts. Notably, Indonesian personal and place names often retain the Indian or Sanskrit pronunciation, with minor adjustments—such as "Vishnu" being pronounced "Wisnu" in Indonesia.

- Sanskrit terms pervade various aspects of Indonesian society. City names, governmental titles, and mottos draw heavily from Sanskrit. For instance, the Indonesian Navy's rank "Laksamana" is derived from *Ramayana* and city awards such as "Adipura" combine Sanskrit roots (Adi meaning "role model" and Pura meaning "city"). Sanskrit phrases also appear in the mottos of the Indonesian military and police forces, emphasizing values rooted in Sanskritic ideals. For example, the police motto *Rashtra Sevakottama* and the Military Academy's motto *Adhitakarya Mahatvavirya Nagarabhakti* demonstrate Sanskrit's continued prestige.

Influence Beyond Asia:

- In ancient and medieval times, Sanskrit words related to food and spices entered European languages, as evidenced by words like "pepper," "ginger," and "sugar" in Greek and Latin. These words eventually spread into English and other European languages, often through trade. During the British Raj, additional Sanskrit words entered English, contributing terms such as "pundit," "guru," "avatar," and "yoga," which are now widely recognized in English and some other European languages.

Modern Sanskrit Usage:

Liturgy, Ceremonies, and Meditation:

Sanskrit remains central to religious liturgy and ceremonial life within Hindu, Buddhist, and Jain traditions. In Hinduism, it is the principal language used in temples and during various rites of passage, such as weddings, baby naming, and cremation ceremonies. Festivals like Durga Puja involve Sanskrit recitations, with entire texts such as the Devi Mahatmya chanted annually, especially in eastern India. In South India, temples like the Meenakshi Temple integrate Sanskrit into their rituals.

Sanskrit's influence is also prominent in Newar Buddhism, where it is the primary language of monastery ceremonies. Mahayana and Tibetan Buddhist scriptures, including sutras, incorporate Sanskrit texts, often alongside vernacular translations. Jainism also utilizes Sanskrit for ritual and doctrinal texts, such as the Tattvartha Sutra and the Bhaktamara Stotra, as well as for mantras recited in ceremonies.

Literature and the Arts:

Since India's independence in 1947, over 3,000 Sanskrit literary works have been composed, with many achieving critical acclaim. The Sahitya Akademi has awarded annual prizes for Sanskrit literature since 1967, and in 2009, Satya Vrat Shastri became the first Sanskrit author to receive the Jnanpith Award, India's highest literary honour.

In music, Sanskrit permeates the Carnatic and Hindustani classical traditions. Kirtanas, bhajans, stotras, and shlokas in Sanskrit are widely cherished. The Samaveda uniquely incorporates musical notation, underscoring the language's foundational role in Indian musical heritage. Sanskrit's influence also extends to contemporary music; for instance, Chinese musician Sa Dingding has produced popular songs in Sanskrit.

Influence in Asia and the West:

Sanskrit loanwords are prevalent across numerous Asian languages, from Filipino and Khmer to Thai and Malay, where it has impacted vocabulary, alphabets, and cultural expression. Old Javanese contains extensive Sanskrit vocabulary, with a dictionary by P.J. Zoetmulder recording over 25,500 entries. English also includes Sanskrit-derived terms introduced through various cultural exchanges.

In the West, Sanskrit education is part of the curriculum at select schools, including St. James Junior School and Avanti Schools Trust in London, where students can study Sanskrit. In the United States, high school students can earn language credits through the Samskrita Bharati's SAFL program. Schools in Australia, New Zealand, and South Africa also offer Sanskrit, making it a globalized language studied by enthusiasts far beyond India.

Jharkhand:

Official Language: Hindi

Additional Official Languages:

Angika:

- **Also Known as**: Anga, Angikar, Chhika-Chhiki.
- **Location**: Spoken in parts of Bihar and Jharkhand, and in Nepal.
- **Relation to Other Languages**: Closely related to Maithili, Bengali, Bhojpuri, and Magahi.
- **Writing Systems**: Historically written in Anga Lipi, then Kaithi Script, now primarily in Devanagari Script.

Bhojpuri:

- **Location**: Spoken in eastern Uttar Pradesh, western Bihar, and northwestern Jharkhand.
- **Population**: About 5% of India's population as of 2000.
- **Relation to Other Languages**: Descendant of Magadhi Prakrit, closely related to Maithili, Magahi, and Bengali.
- **Global Presence**: Minority language in Fiji, Guyana, Mauritius, South Africa, Suriname, and Trinidad and Tobago.
- **Historical Background**: Name derived from Bhojpur, linked to Raja Bhoj. The language has various regional names and variations.

- **Dialectal Variations**: Different names like Buxariya in Mughal armies, Deshwali in Bengal, and Purabiya in Oudh.
- **Linguistic Classification**: Eastern Indo-Aryan language; grouped with Magahi and Maithili as Bihari languages.

Bhumij:

- **Language Family**: Austroasiatic, part of the Munda subfamily.
- **Location**: Spoken in Jharkhand, Odisha, and West Bengal.
- **Current Status**: Extremely endangered; only about 27,506 speakers as per the 2011 census.
- **Writing System**: Historically oral; the Ol Onal script was developed between 1981-1992.

Ho Language:

- **Language Family**: Munda, part of the Austroasiatic language family.
- **Location**: Spoken by the Ho, Munda, Kolha, and Kol communities in Odisha, Jharkhand, Bihar, Chhattisgarh, and West Bengal.
- **Population**: About 2.2 million speakers.
- **Writing Systems**: Primarily written in Warang Citi script; also uses Devanagari, Latin, Odia, and Telugu scripts.

Kharia:

- **Language Family**: Munda, part of the Austroasiatic family.
- **Location**: Spoken in eastern India, particularly in Jharkhand, Chhattisgarh, and Odisha.
- **Linguistic Classification**: Classified with Juang as a subgroup of the South Munda branch.

Khortha:

- **Classification**: Considered a dialect of Magahi.
- **Location**: Primarily spoken in Jharkhand and parts of Bihar.

- **Census Data**: Over 3,11,175 speakers recorded, though actual numbers may be higher.

Kurmali:

- **Classification**: Indo-Aryan language, part of the Bihari group.
- **Location**: Spoken in Jharkhand, Odisha, West Bengal, and Assam.
- **Historical Background**: Known as Panchpargania during the British Raj, referring to trade between five regions.
- **Census Data**: Total of 5,56,089 speakers in India; actual numbers likely higher.

Language Variation:

Kurmali:

- **Region:** Primarily spoken in West Bengal, Jharkhand, and Odisha.
- **Language Shift:** Kurmali speakers, particularly in West Bengal, are shifting towards Bengali due to long-term settlement, affecting their linguistic identity.
- **Historical Classification:** Initially classified under Bengali, now categorized under Hindi since the 1971 census.
- **Lexical Similarity:** Shares significant lexical similarities with Panchpargania, Khortha, Nagpuri, Odia, Bengali, and Hindi.
- **Influence:** The language shows heavy influence from Bengali, leading some linguists to refer to it as Jharkhandi Bangla.
- **Endangerment Status:** Rated as threatened and shifting (EGIDS levels 6b and 7) but classified as vigorous by Ethnologue.

Kurukh:

- **Region:** Spoken mainly in Jharkhand, Chhattisgarh, Odisha, West Bengal, Assam, Bihar, and Tripura.

- **Speakers:** Approximately two million speakers in India and some in Bangladesh, Nepal, and Bhutan.
- **Classification:** Part of the Northern Dravidian group, closely related to the Malto language.
- **Endangerment Status:** Considered vulnerable by UNESCO.
- **Cultural Context:** Used by the Kurukh (Oraon) and Kisan communities, particularly among tea garden workers in West Bengal.

Magahi:

- **Region:** Predominantly spoken in Bihar, Jharkhand, and West Bengal.
- **Historical Context:** Derived from the ancient Magadhi Prakrit and closely linked to the ancient kingdom of Magadha.
- **Speaker Population:** Approximately 20.7 million speakers, including both Magahi and Khortha speakers.
- **Lack of Recognition:** Not constitutionally recognized in India, and absorbed under Hindi in the 1961 Census.
- **Literary Tradition:** Rich in folk songs and oral traditions, though historically it has limited written literature.

Maithili:

- **Region:** Native to the Mithila region of Bihar and parts of Nepal.
- **Recognition:** One of the 22 official languages of India and the second most spoken language in Nepal.
- **Scripts:** Primarily written in Devanagari, with historical scripts like Tirhuta and Kaithi.
- **Cultural Significance:** Maithili literature dates back to the Charyapadas and has a rich tradition of poetry and folk culture.
- **Official Status:** Gained recognition in 2002 as a major Indian language, included in the Eighth Schedule of the Indian Constitution.

Mundari:

- **Region:** Spoken by Munda tribes in Jharkhand, Odisha, and West Bengal.
- **Relation to Other Languages:** Closely related to Santali; part of the Austroasiatic language family.
- **Writing Systems:** Uses Mundari Bani script, Devanagari, Odia, Bengali, and Latin scripts.
- **Historical Context:** Linguistically tied to Munda migration patterns and Indo-Aryan influences.
- **Speaker Population:** At least 1.1 million speakers in the stated regions, with additional speakers recorded under "Munda."

Nagpuri:

- **Also Known as**: Sadri, Nagpuria.
- **Region**: Spoken in Jharkhand, Chhattisgarh, Odisha, and Bihar, primarily in the Chota Nagpur plateau.
- **Ethnic Group**: Native language of the Sadan, an Indo-Aryan ethnic group.
- **Usage**:
    - Lingua franca for tribal groups (Kurukh, Kharia, Munda).
    - Adopted by the Tea-garden community in Assam and West Bengal.
- **Speakers**: Approximately 5.1 million native speakers (2011 Census); about 7 million second-language speakers (2007 study).
- **Linguistic Classification**: Considered a dialect of Bhojpuri by some; distinct from other Indo-Aryan languages.
- **Literary Tradition**: Rich in folk tales and songs; evidence of literature since the 17th century.
- **Prominent Writers**: Includes poets like Hanuman Singh, Ghasi Ram Mahli, and historical works such as "Nagvanshavali."
- **Historical Background**:

- Classified as Nagpuria dialect by Sir George Abraham Grierson in 1903.
- Influenced by various forms of Prakrit and considered a descendant of Magadhi Prakrit.

Odia:

- **Formerly Known as**: Oriya.
- **Region**: Official language of Odisha; also spoken in parts of West Bengal, Jharkhand, Andhra Pradesh, and Chhattisgarh.
- **Population**: 82% of Odisha's population are native speakers.
- **Language Classification**: Eastern Indo-Aryan language, evolved from Odra Prakrit.
- **Classical Status**: Designated as a classical language for its long literary history and minimal influence from Persian and Arabic.
- **Historical Development**:
  - Proto Odia (10th century and earlier).
  - Old Odia (10th to 13th centuries).
  - Early Middle Odia (13th to 15th centuries).
  - Middle Odia (15th to 17th centuries).
  - Late Middle Odia (17th century to early 19th century).
  - Modern Odia (late 19th century to present).
- **Key Figures**: Prominent writers include Upendra Bhanja, Fakir Mohan Senapati, and Madhusudan Das.
- **Cultural Significance**: Known for its rich literary tradition, with various genres represented from poetry to prose.

Odia Language:

Geographical Distribution:

- **India**: Primarily spoken in Odisha, with significant populations in:

- **Neighbouring States**: Andhra Pradesh, Madhya Pradesh, Jharkhand, West Bengal, Chhattisgarh.
- **Other Regions**: Gujarat (due to labor migration), and cities like Vishakhapatnam, Hyderabad, Bangalore, Mumbai, etc.

- **Speaker Statistics**: 3.1% of Indians are Odia speakers (2011 Census); 93% from Odisha.

Foreign Presence:

- **Odia Diaspora**: Approximately 50 million speakers worldwide.
- **Countries**: Significant communities in Thailand, Indonesia, USA, Canada, Australia, England, and others.

Literature:

- **Origins**: Earliest literature traced to **Charyapadas** (7th-9th centuries).
- **Key Works**:
    - **14th Century**: Sarala Das wrote the **Sarala Mahabharata** and **Chandi Purana**.
    - **Panchasakha Age**: Adaptation of Sanskrit texts; prominent poets include Balarama Dasa and Jagannatha Dasa.
    - **Bhanja Age (1700-1850)**: Characterized by complex language and eroticism; notable poet: Upendra Bhanja.
- **Modern Era**: Emergence of historical novels and modern drama; significant writers include:
    - **20th Century**: Fakir Mohan Senapati, Muralidhar Mallick, and Chintamani Das.
    - **Contemporary**: Manoj Das, Rabi Patnaik, and Pratibha Ray; noted poets like Kabibar Radhanath Ray and Sitakanta Mohapatra.

Santali Language:

Geographical Distribution:

- **India**: Primarily in Jharkhand, West Bengal, Odisha, Bihar, Assam, and other states.
- **Speaker Statistics**: Over 7 million speakers in India (2011 Census), primarily in Jharkhand (2.75 million) and West Bengal (2.43 million).
- **International Presence**: Spoken in parts of Bangladesh, Bhutan, and Nepal.

Historical Background:

- **Origins**: Oral language until the 19th century; first documented by European missionaries.
- **Writing Systems**: Initially used Bengali, Odia, and Roman scripts; the **Ol Chiki script** was developed in 1925 by Raghunath Murmu.

Literature:

- **Development**: Early literature consisted of folk tales; documentation efforts in the 19th century led to dictionaries and studies.
- **Ol Chiki Acceptance**: Gained acceptance as the official script in parts of India.

Urdu: Mentioned above

Karnataka:

Official Language:

Kannada:

Kannada, also known historically as Canarese, is a Dravidian language primarily spoken in Karnataka, a state in southwestern India. It boasts around 44 million native speakers and is also a second or third language for approximately 15 million non-native speakers in the region.

Historical Significance: Kannada has served as the court language for several prominent dynasties in southern and central India, including the Kadambas, Chalukyas, Rashtrakutas, Yadava Dynasty, Western Ganga dynasty, Wodeyars of Mysore, Nayakas of Keladi, Hoysalas, and the Vijayanagara Empire. The language holds official status in Karnataka and is recognized as a scheduled language in India, further classified among the designated classical languages of the country.

Script and Linguistic Features: The Kannada language is written using the Kannada script, which evolved from the 5th-century Kadamba script. Kannada has a long epigraphic history of around 1,500 years, with literary Old Kannada flourishing during the 6th-century Ganga dynasty and the 9th-century Rashtrakuta Dynasty. Its literary heritage extends over a millennium, contributing to Kannada literature being awarded eight Jnanapith awards—the most for any Dravidian language.

In July 2011, a center dedicated to classical Kannada studies was established at the Central Institute of Indian Languages in Mysore to facilitate research and promote the language.

Geographical Distribution: According to the 2011 census, Kannada had 43.5 million native speakers in India, with 40.6 million residing in Karnataka—about two-thirds of the state's population. Notable populations of native Kannada speakers also exist in neighboring states:

- **Tamil Nadu:** 1,140,000 speakers
- **Maharashtra:** 993,000 speakers
- **Andhra Pradesh/Telangana:** 533,000 speakers
- **Kerala:** 78,100 speakers
- **Goa:** 67,800 speakers

Outside India, Kannada is spoken in various countries, including:

- **United States:** 48,600 speakers (2015 census)
- **Canada:** 4,000 speakers (2016 census)
- **Australia:** 9,700 speakers (2016 census)
- **Singapore:** 22,000 speakers (2018 estimate)

- **Malaysia:** 59,000 speakers (2021 estimate)

Linguistic Evolution: Kannada is classified as a Southern Dravidian language and its history is typically divided into three stages:

- **Old Kannada (Haḷegannaḍa):** 450 to 1200 AD
- **Middle Kannada (Naḍugannaḍa):** 1200 to 1700 AD
- **Modern Kannada (Hosagannaḍa):** 1700 to present

The language has been influenced by Sanskrit and Prakrit significantly. According to scholar Iravatham Mahadevan, Kannada had a rich spoken tradition as early as the 3rd century BC. K. V. Narayana also suggests that various tribal languages, now classified as Kannada dialects, might reflect earlier forms of the language with less external influence.

Influences from Other Languages: The grammatical framework of literary Kannada appears to be shaped by three main sources:

- **Pāṇini's Grammar**
- **Non-Pāṇinian Schools of Sanskrit Grammar:** Particularly the Katantra and Sakatayana schools.
- **Prakrit Grammar**

Throughout history, vernacular Prakrit speakers have influenced Kannada, leading to naturalized words in Kannada. For example, **baṇṇa** (color) is derived from **vaṇṇa**, and **huṇṇime** (full moon) from **puṇṇivā**. Kannada also incorporates Sanskrit-origin words, such as **varṇa** (color) and **rāya** (king), showcasing its diverse linguistic roots.

Literature:

Overview of Kannada Language:

- **Classification**: Kannada is a Dravidian language predominantly spoken in Karnataka, India, with a significant number of speakers in neighboring states.
- **Speakers**: Approximately 44 million native speakers, with

an additional 15 million speaking it as a second or third language.

- **Status**: Official language of Karnataka, designated as a classical language in India.

Historical Development:

1. Old Kannada (Haḷegannaḍa):

- Earliest known record: Kappe Arabhatta (7th century).
- Notable work: **Kavirajamarga** by King Amoghavarsha I, focusing on literary criticism.
- **Vaḍḍārādhane** (900 AD): A prose work describing Bhadrabahu's life.
- Early poets and writers mentioned include Durvinita and Ravikirti, but many works are now lost.

2. Middle Kannada (Naḍugannaḍa):

- Flourished between the 15th and 18th centuries.
- Major influence of Hinduism and the advent of devotional poetry, particularly **Haridasa Sahitya** (Dasa literature).
- Notable figure: **Kumara Vyasa**, known for adapting the Mahabharata into Kannada.

3. Modern Kannada (Hosagannaḍa):

- Transitioned in the 19th century, marked by notable works like *Indira Bai* and contributions from poets like Nandalike Muddana.
- Printing began with significant works like **Canarese Grammar** (1817) and the **Bible in Canarese** (1820).
- Influenced by various literary movements (Navodaya, Dalita, etc.) in the 20th century.
- Contemporary authors include Kuvempu and V K Gokak.

Literary Contributions:

- **Jnanapith Awards**: Kannada literature has received the highest number of these awards among Indian languages, reflecting its rich literary tradition.
- **Genres**: Development of various literary forms including folk poetry, prosody, and devotional literature.

Cultural Impact:

- The Vachana Sahitya tradition reflects social and religious conditions, with contributions from figures like Basavanna and Akka Mahadevi.
- The language has retained its distinct identity, balancing between traditional and modern influences.

Kerala:

Official Language: Malyalam:

General Information:

- **Language Family**: Dravidian language.
- **Region**: Spoken primarily in Kerala and the union territories of Lakshadweep and Puducherry (Mahé).
- **Speakers**: Approximately 34 million people, including linguistic minorities in neighboring states and the Malayali diaspora worldwide.
- **Status**: Official language in Kerala, Lakshadweep, and Puducherry; recognized as a "Classical Language of India" in 2013.
- **Geographical Distribution**:
    - ♦ Spoken primarily in Kerala, Lakshadweep, and Puducherry (Mahé).
    - ♦ Spoken by about 34 million people, including diaspora communities worldwide, especially in the Persian Gulf.

- **Language Classification**:
  - A Dravidian language and one of the 22 scheduled languages of India.
  - Designated a "Classical Language of India" in 2013.
- **Historical Origins**:
  - Evolved from early Middle Tamil, separating around the 9th century CE.
  - Oldest known inscription: Quilon Syrian copper plates (849/850 CE).
  - Earliest literary work: *Ramacharitam* (late 12th or early 13th century).
- **Scripts:**
  - Originally written in the Vatteluttu script.
  - Current script evolved from Vatteluttu and Grantha scripts, incorporating Indo-Aryan loanwords.
- **Language Development**:
  - Old Malayalam (9th to 13th century) marked the initial divergence from Tamil.
  - Middle Malayalam (13th to 15th century) saw the emergence of distinct literature and influences from Sanskrit and Manipravalam.
  - Modern Malayalam (from the 15th century) developed into its current form with contributions from poets like Thunchaththu Ezhuthachan.
- **Cultural Context**:
  - Influenced by the geographical isolation of Kerala and the arrival of immigrant communities.
  - Significant literary contributions from figures like Kunchan Nambiar and later, the Modern Triumvirate (Kumaran Asan, Ulloor S. Parameswara Iyer, and Vallathol Narayana Menon).
- **Linguistic Features**:
  - Shares many innovations with Tamil but also has unique archaic features not found in Tamil.

- Has borrowed extensively from Arabic and European languages due to historical trade relations.
- **Significance in Literature**:
  - The Sangam literature is considered a predecessor.
  - Modern literature flourished in the 19th and 20th centuries with numerous acclaimed authors.

Linguistic Features:

- **Scripts**: Evolved from the Vatteluttu script, incorporating Grantha script for Indo-Aryan loanwords; influenced by the Tigalari script.
- **Linguistic Characteristics**: Distinct from Tamil, including nasalization, vowel contraction, and other phonetic features.
- **Influences**: Strong impact from Sanskrit and Prakrit due to geographical and cultural factors.

Literature:

- **Historical Works**: Earliest literary works date back to the 12th century (e.g., *Ramacharitam*).
- **Influential Figures**:
  - Thunchaththu Ezhuthachan: credited with modernizing the script.
  - Kunchan Nambiar: introduced Thullal, a new literary form.
  - Notable modern writers: G. Sankara Kurup, M. T. Vasudevan Nair, Kamala Das, and others.
- **Modern Developments**: Prose literature and journalism flourished in the late 18th century, leading to contemporary literary movements.

Cultural Context:

- **Trade Influence**: Significant borrowing of words from Arabic and European languages due to historical trade interactions.

- **Sangam Literature**: Considered a predecessor to Malayalam literature, reflecting early cultural and linguistic connections.

Types of Early Malayalam Literature:

- **Malayalam Nada**: Traditional compositions in the Malayalam language.
- **Tamil Nada**: Influence from Tamil literary traditions.
- **Sanskrit Nada**: Integration of Sanskrit elements.

Notable Forms of Composition:

- **Nadan Pattu**: Classical songs in Malayalam.
- **Manipravalam**: A hybrid of Sanskrit and Malayalam; prominent in 14th-century poetry by poets like Madhava Panikkar and Sankara Panikkar.
- **Folk Songs**: Rich in native elements, these songs were primarily oral and connected to cultural practices, including agricultural activities.

Influential Poets:

- **15th-16th Century**:
  - Cherusseri Namboothiri
  - Thunchaththu Ezhuthachan (known as the father of modern Malayalam literature)
  - Poonthanam Nambudiri
- **17th-18th Century**:
  - Unnayi Variyar
  - Kunchan Nambiar (notable for the Thullal literary form).

Historical Context:

- **Arabi Malayalam**: Early works (16th-17th centuries) contain vocabulary close to modern Malayalam.
- **Prose Development**: Began in the latter half of the 18th century; journalism emerged.

- **Cultural Themes**: Contemporary literature addresses social, political, and economic contexts.

Key Literary Works:

- **Ramacharitam & Vaishikatantram**: The earliest known examples of Pattu and Manipravalam from the 12th century.
- **Bhashakautalyam**: The earliest extant prose work, a commentary in simple Malayalam.
- **Adhyatmaramayanam**: A significant work by Ezhuthachan.
- **Unnunili Sandesam**: Among the oldest literary works in Malayalam from the 14th century.

Evolution of Malayalam:

- **Old & Middle Malayalam**:
- Earliest poems (12th-14th centuries) predating Sanskrit alphabet introduction.
- Campu form (14th century) blended poetry and prose with Sanskrit influence.
- Notable works from this period include *Unniyachi Charitham* and *Unnichirudevi Charitham*.

Modern Malayalam:

- **Krishnagatha**: Written by Cherusseri Namboothiri; considered the first literary work in modern spoken Malayalam.
- **Later Influences**: Ezhuthachan and Poonthanam contributed to modern poetry in the 16th century, with themes and language reflecting contemporary spoken Malayalam.
- **Keralolpathi**: Attributed to Ezhuthachan, narrating the Parashurama legend.

Cultural Impact:

- **Folk Songs**: Represent the oldest literary form in Malayalam, often linked to agricultural themes and oral traditions.

- **Geographical Influence**: The Bharathappuzha river basin significantly shaped the evolution of Malayalam literature.

Contributions of European Scholars:

- **Graham Shaw**: Published the *Malabar English Dictionary* (1779), initially a Tamil-English dictionary.
- **Paremmakkal Thoma Kathanar**: Authored *Varthamanappusthakam*, the first Malayalam travelogue (1789).
- **Hermann Gundert**: A German missionary who significantly advanced Malayalam literature by:
  - Writing foundational texts such as *Keralolpathi*, *Pazhancholmala*, and *Malayalabhaasha Vyakaranam*.
  - Creating *Paathamala*, the first Malayalam school textbook.
  - Producing *Kerala Pazhama*, the first Malayalam dictionary, and the first Malayalam newspaper, *Rajya Samacharam* (1847).
  - Translating the Bible into Malayalam and living in Thalassery for 20 years.

Institutional Developments:

- **Church Mission Society (CMS)**: Established a seminary in Kottayam (1819) and initiated printing in Malayalam.
- **Benjamin Bailey**: Anglican priest who made the first Malayalam types and contributed to prose standardization.
- **Marthomite Movement**: In the mid-19th century, called for replacing Syriac with Malayalam in church liturgy, leading to the latter's adoption by the end of the century.

Literary Milestones (1900-1950):

- **Vengayil Kunhiraman Nayanar**: Authored the first Malayalam short story, *Vasanavikriti*.

- **O. Chandu Menon**: Wrote *Indulekha* and *Saradha*, with *Indulekha* being the first major Malayalam novel.
- **Venmani School**: A new poetic movement in the 19th century focused on common life themes and the use of pure Malayalam (Pachcha Malayalam). Notable poets include:
    - Venmani Achhan Nambudiripad
    - Poonthottam Achhan Nambudiri
    - Kodungallur Kunjikkuttan Thampuran

20th Century Developments:

- **Prominent Poets and Writers**: Jnanpith winners and influential figures include:
    - G. Sankara Kurup
    - Thakazhi Sivasankara Pillai
    - M. T. Vasudevan Nair
    - O. N. V. Kurup
    - Vaikom Muhammad Basheer
- **Travelogue Literature**: S. K. Pottekkatt's works were pivotal in this genre.
- **Drama**: Writers like Kavalam Narayana Panicker made significant contributions.
- **Non-political Literature**: Thakazhi's *Chemmeen*, Basheer's *Pathummayude Aadu*, and P. C. Kuttikrishnan's *Ummachu* focused on social and domestic themes.

Evolution of Fiction and Poetry:

- **New Prose Forms**: The 1950s saw innovative narratives from Basheer and M. T. Vasudevan Nair, signaling a shift in fiction.

- **Political Themes in Poetry**: Contemporary Malayalam poetry often reflects social, political, and economic issues with a tendency towards radicalism.
- **Media Exposure**: Kerala has the highest media presence in India, with newspapers in multiple languages, primarily Malayalam and English.

Additional Official Language: English

Madhya Pradesh:

Official Language: Hindi

Maharashtra:

Official Language:

Marathi Language and Literature:

- **Language Background**:
  - Marathi is an Indo-Aryan language spoken primarily in Maharashtra, India.
  - Official language of Maharashtra and Goa, with around 83 million speakers (2011).
  - It has a three-way gender system and unique pronoun distinctions.
- **Historical Development**:
  - Evolved from Maharashtri Prakrit, with inscriptions dating back to the 1st century BCE.
  - The first notable prose work, *Vivēkasindhu*, was written by Mukundaraja.
- **Yadava and Medieval Periods**:
  - Increased literary output during the Yadava dynasty (12th century).

  - Key works include Dnyaneshwar's *Dnyaneshwari* and Eknath's devotional writings.
- **Sultanate Period and Maratha Empire**:
  - Marathi was promoted for administration during the Sultanate period.
  - Under Chhatrapati Shivaji Maharaj, Marathi became the court language.
  - Flourished in literature, including *Powada* and *Lavani*.
- **Colonial Era**:
  - Standardization of grammar occurred under British influence.
  - The first Marathi newspaper, *Durpan*, was published in 1832.
- **Post-Independence Developments**:
  - Recognized as a scheduled language after Indian independence.
  - The formation of Maharashtra in 1960 boosted literary growth.
  - Notable authors include Khandekar, Tendulkar, and P.L. Deshpande.
- **Dalit Literature Movement**:
  - Emerged in the late 20th century, inspired by social reformers.
  - Key figures include Baburao Bagul and Namdeo Dhasal, addressing marginalized voices.
- **Contemporary Concerns**:
  - Increasing use of English medium schools raises concerns about the marginalization of Marathi.

Geographic Distribution of Marathi:

- **Primary Regions**:
  - **Maharashtra**: The main state where Marathi is spoken.
  - **Goa**: Significant Marathi-speaking population.
- **Neighboring States**:

    - **Gujarat**: Mainly in Vadodara and a small population in Surat.
    - **Madhya Pradesh**: In districts like Burhanpur, Betul, Chhindwara, and Balaghat.
    - **Karnataka**: Spoken in Belagavi, Karwar, Bagalkote, Vijayapura, Kalaburagi, and Bidar.
    - **Chhattisgarh**: Presence of Marathi speakers.
    - **Tamil Nadu**: In Thanjavur.
    - **Telangana**: Small Marathi-speaking communities.
- **Union Territories**:
    - Daman and Diu
    - Dadra and Nagar Haveli
- **Historical Context**:
    - Cities like Baroda, Indore, Gwalior, Jabalpur, and Tanjore have historically had sizeable Marathi-speaking populations due to Maratha rule.
- **Overseas Communities**:
    - Marathi is spoken by Maharashtrian migrants, notably in Mauritius since the early 19th century.
- **Population Statistics**:
    - Approximately 83 million native speakers as of the 2011 census, making Marathi the third most spoken native language in India (6.86% of the total population).
    - Distribution in India:
        - **Maharashtra**: 70.34%
        - **Goa**: 10.89%
        - **Dadra and Nagar Haveli**: 7.01%
        - **Daman and Diu**: 4.53%
        - **Karnataka**: 3.38%
        - **Madhya Pradesh**: 1.7%
        - **Gujarat**: 1.52%

Manipur:

Official Language:

Meitei (Manipuri):

- **Language Family**: Tibeto-Burman language, part of the Sino-Tibetan language family.
- **Status**: Official language of Manipur and one of the official languages of India.
- **Speakers**:
    - Approximately 1.76 million native speakers as of the 2011 census.
    - 1.52 million speakers in Manipur, where they represent a majority.
    - Smaller populations in Assam (168,000), Tripura (24,000), Nagaland (9,500), and other parts of India (37,500).
    - Spoken by communities in Myanmar and Bangladesh.

Linguistic Classification:

- **Subgroup**: Belongs to the Kamarupan group of Tibeto-Burman languages.
- **Historical Classification**: Previously classified in various groups, current consensus places it as its own subdivision, though some still link it to Kuki-Chin-Naga.

Historical Context:

- **Ancient Roots**: The Meitei language has existed for over 2000 years, with early compositions like the ritual song "Ougri" and the epic "Numit Kappa."
- **First Millennium CE**: Significant literary works, such as "Poireiton Khunthok" and "Khencho," were composed.
- **Second Millennium CE**:

- ♦ Experienced Hindu cultural influences from the late 17th century.
- ♦ Shift from traditional script to Bengali-Assamese script initiated by King Pamheiba, along with the creation of Hindu literature in Meitei.

Geographical Distribution:

- **Primary Area**: Majority of speakers (1.5 million) reside in Manipur; it serves as the official language and lingua franca.
- **Neighboring States**: Significant populations in Assam, Nagaland, and smaller communities in Tripura and elsewhere.
- **International Presence**: Approximately 15,000 speakers in Bangladesh and communities in Myanmar (Kachin and Shan states).

Nomenclature:

- **Alternate Names**: Includes Kathe, Kathi, Meetei, Meiteilon, and others.
- **Preferred Name**: Many native speakers prefer "Meitei" or its variant "Meithei" over "Manipuri," derived from the term for the language (Meitheirón).
- **Loconyms**: "Manipuri" is commonly used to refer to the language and the people of Manipur.

Cultural Significance:

- **Safety and Vulnerability**: Assessed as a safe language by Ethnologue (EGIDS level 2), but considered vulnerable by UNESCO.
- **Literary Status**: Recognized as an advanced literary language by Sahitya Akademi, India's National Academy of Letters.

Additional Official Language: English

Meghalaya:

Official Language: English

Additional Official Languages: Khasi and Garo

Khasi:

- **Language Family**: Khasi is an Austroasiatic language.
- **Speakers**: Over 1 million speakers, primarily among the Khasi people in Meghalaya, India.
- **Status**: Holds associate official status in some districts of Meghalaya.

Geographic Distribution:

- **Native Speakers**: Approximately 1,038,000 people as of the 2011 census.
    - ♦ Khasi is the first language for about one-third of Meghalaya's population (around 997,000 speakers).
    - ♦ Predominantly spoken in the Khasi Hills and Jaintia Hills regions.
    - ♦ Smaller communities exist in neighboring states, particularly Assam (34,600 speakers) and a few in Bangladesh.
- **Official Recognition**: Became an associate official language in Meghalaya in 2005; UNESCO no longer considers it endangered as of 2012. There are calls to include Khasi in the Eighth Schedule of the Indian Constitution.

Literature and Culture:

- **Literary Presence**: A significant number of books have been published in Khasi, including novels, poetry, religious texts, school textbooks, and non-fiction.

- **Prominent Figure**: U Soso Tham, a renowned Khasi poet, is commemorated annually as a regional holiday in Meghalaya.
- **Digital Presence**: Khasi has a notable presence online, including blogs and newspapers.

Dialects:

- **Dialects of Khasi**: Significant dialectal variation includes:
    - Sohra Khasi
    - Mylliem Khasi
    - Mawlai Khasi
    - Nongkrem Khasi
    - War Khasi
    - Bhoi Khasi
    - Nonglung
- **Classification Challenges**:
    - Some dialects, such as Pnar, Maram (including Langrin), and Lyngngam, are considered sister languages rather than dialects of Khasi.
    - Bhoi and Nonglung are distinct enough to be viewed as separate languages by some linguists.
    - Sohra dialect is regarded as Standard Khasi due to its early use in Latin and Bengali scripts by the British.
- **Variation**: Standard Khasi is spoken mainly in Shillong but differs from other local dialects that create a dialect continuum.

Khasi is a vibrant language with a rich literary tradition and a significant number of speakers, primarily in Meghalaya. Its dialectal variations reflect its complex linguistic landscape, and its official recognition underscores its importance in the region's cultural identity.

Garo:

- **Language Family**: Garo is a Tibeto-Burman language, part of the Baric group within the Sino-Tibetan language family.
- **Endonym**: Locally referred to as A·chikku.
- **Speakers**: Approximately 889,000 speakers in India (as per the 2001 census) and around 130,000 in Bangladesh.

Geographic Distribution:

- **Primary Regions**:
  - Garo Hills in Meghalaya
  - Areas of Assam (Goalpara, Kamrup, Sivasagar, Karbi Anglong)
  - Nagaland (Kohima district)
  - Tripura (Udaipur subdivision, North and West Tripura districts)
  - Parts of West Bengal (Jalpaiguri, Koch Bihar)
  - Various districts in Bangladesh (Mymensingh, Sunamganj, Sylhet, etc.)

Linguistic Affiliation:

- **Subgroup**: Garo is closely related to other languages in the Boro-Garo subgroup, including Boro, Kokborok, Dimasa, Rabha, and Atong.
- **Common Features**: These languages share many linguistic characteristics, making them somewhat mutually intelligible at a surface level.

Orthography and Standardization:

- **Writing System**: Initially written using Bengali script; now primarily uses a Latin-based alphabet developed by American missionaries.
- **Alphabet**: The current Garo alphabet consists of 20 letters and includes a raised dot (rakga) representing a glottal stop.

- **Historical Context**: The switch to the Latin alphabet was completed by 1924. There's still some use of Bengali script in Bangladesh.
- **Modern Influences**: The language has absorbed vocabulary from Bengali, Assamese, English, and Hindi, particularly in urban areas.

Dialects:

- **Major Dialects**:
  - ♦ **A·we**: Predominantly spoken in Garo Hills.
  - ♦ **Am·beng**: Found across a wide area, including parts of Assam and Bangladesh.
  - ♦ **Atong, Ruga, Chibok, Me·gam**, and several others, each associated with specific geographic regions.
- **Mutual Intelligibility**: Dialects can generally be understood by each other, though some may require explanation for unique words and expressions.
- **Standard vs. Traditional**: Distinction exists between Standard A·we (associated with Tura) and Traditional A·we (spoken in more rural areas).

Status and Use:

- **Official Recognition**: Garo is an associate official language in the Garo Hills districts of Meghalaya (2005).
- **Education**: Used as a medium of instruction in elementary schools; taught as a subject in secondary schools. Higher education options include a B.A. (Honours) in Garo at North-Eastern Hill University.
- **Literary Growth**: There has been significant growth in Garo literature, including dictionaries, textbooks, novels, and religious texts.

Garo is a vital language for the Garo people, with a rich cultural heritage and growing educational and literary presence. Its continued use and development in formal settings contribute to its significance in the northeastern Indian linguistic landscape.

Mizoram:

Official Language:

Mizo:

- **Language Family**: Mizo is a Tibeto-Burman language belonging to the Sino-Tibetan family.
- **Endonyms**: Locally known as **Zohnahthlâk ṭawngho** or **Mizo ṭawngho**.
- **Colonial Name**: Previously referred to as **Duhlian** or **Lushai**; the term Lushai originates from the Duhlian people, who were among the first encountered by the British.

Geographic Distribution:

- **Primary Regions**:
  - **India**: Official language in Mizoram; also spoken in Meghalaya, Manipur, Tripura, and Assam.
  - **Myanmar**: Spoken in Sagaing Region and Chin State.
  - **Bangladesh**: Found in the Chittagong Hill Tracts.

Speaker Population:

- **Total Speakers**: Approximately 850,000 speakers.
  - **India**: 830,846 (2011 Census)
  - **Bangladesh**: 1,041 (1981 Census)
  - **Myanmar**: 12,500 (1983 Census)

Linguistic Features:

- **Dialects**: While based on the **Lusei dialect**, Mizo incorporates vocabulary from various surrounding Mizo clans, contributing to its linguistic richness.
- **Relation to Other Languages**: Mizo shares a significant number of words with other languages in the **Kuki-Chin-Mizo** subgroup, facilitating mutual understanding among speakers of these related languages.

Status and Use:

- **Official Language**: Mizo is the official language of Mizoram, serving as a lingua franca among various ethnic groups within the state.
- **Cultural Importance**: As the mother tongue of the Mizo people, it plays a crucial role in preserving their identity and cultural heritage.

Mizo is an integral language for the Mizo people, with a rich historical context and a diverse linguistic heritage. Its widespread use across multiple states and its official status in Mizoram underscore its importance in the region.

Additional Officail Language: English

Nagaland:

Official Language: English

Odisha:

Odia Language: Odia

Odia:

- **Language Family**: Odia (formerly known as Oriya) is an **Eastern Indo-Aryan** language within the **Indo-Aryan** language family.
- **Status**: It is one of the **official languages of India** and is recognized as a **classical language** due to its long literary history and limited borrowing from other languages.

Historical Context:

- **Origins**: Odia descends from **Odra Prakrit**, which evolved from **Magadhi Prakrit**, the language used in early Jain and Buddhist texts. The earliest known inscriptions in Odia date back to the **10th century CE**.

Historical Eras of Odia Language:

A. **Proto-Odia (Odra Prakrit)** (10th century and earlier): Early inscriptions show the evolution of Odra Prakrit words alongside Sanskrit.

B. **Old Odia** (10th–13th century): Marked by inscriptions like the **Urajam inscription** from 1051 CE.

C. **Early Middle Odia** (13th–15th century): The **Madala Panji** from the Jagannath Temple at Puri is one of the earliest prose examples.

D. **Middle Odia** (15th–17th century): Notable works include **Mahabharata** and **Bilanka Ramayana** by **Sarala Das.**

E. **Late Middle Odia** (17th century–Early 19th century): Featured prominent poets like **Upendra Bhanja**, known for significant literary contributions.

F. **Modern Odia** (Late 19th century to present): The first Odia magazine, **Bodha Dayini**, was published in 1861, marking a significant period of literature and journalism.

Geographical Distribution:

- **India**:
  - Predominantly spoken in **Odisha**, where it is the official language.
  - Significant populations in **Andhra Pradesh**, **Madhya Pradesh**, **Jharkhand**, **West Bengal**, and **Chhattisgarh**.
  - Notable speakers in cities like **Vishakhapatnam**, **Hyderabad**, **Mumbai**, and **New Delhi**.
- **Global Presence**:
  - Worldwide, the Odia diaspora is estimated to include **50 million speakers**, with communities in **Thailand**, **Indonesia**, **the USA**, **Canada**, **Australia**, and parts of **the Middle East**.

Dialects and Varieties:

Major Varieties:

1. **Baleswari** (Northern Odia): Spoken in northern Odisha and parts of West Bengal.
2. **Kataki** (Central Odia): Found in the coastal and central regions of Odisha.
3. **Khurda Odia**: Primarily spoken in Khordha, Puri, and Nayagarh districts.
4. **Ganjami** (Southern Odia): Spoken in southern Odisha and parts of Andhra Pradesh.
5. **Sundargadi** (Northwestern Odia): Found in Sundergarh and adjacent districts.
6. **Sambalpuri** (Western Odia): Spoken in western districts of Odisha and parts of Chhattisgarh.
7. **Desia** (Southwestern Odia/Koraputi): Found in south western Odisha and parts of Andhra Pradesh.

Minor Dialects and Sociolects:

- **Medinipuri Odia**: In West Bengal.
- **Singhbhumi Odia**: In Jharkhand.
- **Bodo Parja, Bhatri, Reli, Kupia**: Tribal dialects in Odisha and neighbouring states.

Cultural Significance:

Odia serves as a crucial marker of identity for the people of Odisha and has a rich literary tradition that spans centuries. The language continues to thrive through its literature, media, and educational institutions, contributing to its preservation and growth in modern contexts.

Minor Regional Dialects:

A. **Medinipuri Odia (Medinipuria)**:

- **Location**: Parts of undivided Midnapore district and Kakdwip subdivision (South 24 Parganas) in West Bengal.

B. **Singhbhumi Odia**:

- **Location**: East Singhbhum, West Singhbhum, and Saraikela-Kharsawan districts in Jharkhand.

C. **Phulbani Odia**:

- **Location**: Kandhamal district and parts of Boudh district in Odisha.

D. **Kalahandia Odia**:

- **Location**: Kalahandi and Nuapada districts, as well as neighboring districts in Chhattisgarh.

E. **Debagadia Odia**:

- **Location**: Spoken in Debagarh district and adjacent areas like Rairakhol and Athmallik; also known as Debgadia or Deogarhia.

Major Tribal and Community Dialects/Sociolects:

A. **Bodo Parja (Jharia)**:

- **Spoken by**: Parang Proja tribe in Koraput and surrounding districts of Odisha.

B. **Bhatri**:

- **Spoken by**: Bhottada tribe in Odisha and parts of Chhattisgarh.

C. **Reli**:

- **Spoken by**: Reli community in Koraput and Rayagada districts of southern Odisha and neighboring Andhra Pradesh.

D. **Kupia**:

- **Spoken by**: Valmiki people primarily in Koraput and Visakhapatnam districts.

Minor Sociolects:

A. **Bhuyan**:

- **Type**: Tribal dialect spoken in Northern Odisha.

B. **Kurmi**:

- **Location**: Northern Odisha and southwestern Bengal.

C. **Sounti**:
  - **Location**: Northern Odisha and southwestern Bengal.

D. **Bathudi**:
  - **Location**: Northern Odisha and southwestern Bengal.

E. **Kondhan**:
  - **Type**: Tribal dialect spoken in Western Odisha.

F. **Agharia**:
  - **Spoken by**: Agharia community in Western Odisha and parts of Chhattisgarh.

G. **Bhulia**:
  - **Spoken by**: Bhulia community in districts of Western Odisha and Chhattisgarh.

H. **Matia**:
  - **Type**: Tribal dialect spoken in Southern Odisha.

The diversity within the Odia language includes a variety of minor regional dialects, each with its unique characteristics tied to specific geographical locations. Additionally, the major tribal and community dialects reflect the rich cultural tapestry of the Odia-speaking population, showcasing the language's adaptability and significance across different communities. These dialects play an essential role in preserving local cultures and identities while contributing to the overall richness of the Odia linguistic landscape.

Additional Official Language: English

Punjab:

Official Language: Punjabi

Punjabi, also spelled Panjabi, is an **Indo-Aryan language** native to the Punjab region of Pakistan and India. With approximately **113 million native speakers**, it is one of the most widely spoken languages globally.

- **In Pakistan**: Punjabi is the most widely spoken first language, with **80.5 million speakers** (39% of the population) as per the 2017 census.
- **In India**: Punjabi ranks as the 11th most widely spoken language, with **31.1 million speakers** according to the 2011 census.
- **Diaspora**: Significant Punjabi-speaking communities exist in **Canada**, the **United Kingdom**, the **United States**, **Australia**, and the **Gulf states**.

Writing Systems:

- In **Pakistan**, Punjabi is written using the **Shahmukhi alphabet**, based on the Perso-Arabic script.
- In **India**, it is written using the **Gurmukhi alphabet**, based on Indic scripts.

Unique Feature:

Punjabi is notable for its use of **lexical tone**, a rarity among Indo-Aryan languages and the broader Indo-European family.

History:

Etymology:

The term "Punjabi" is derived from **Panj-āb**, Persian for 'Five Waters', referencing the five major eastern tributaries of the Indus River. The name was introduced by **Turko-Persian conquerors** and translated from the Sanskrit name **Panchanada**, meaning 'Land of the Five Rivers'.

- **Panj**: Cognate with Sanskrit **pañca** (five), Greek **pénte**, and Lithuanian **Penki**.
- **Āb**: Cognate with Sanskrit **áp** and the Av- of **Avon**.

Origin:

Punjabi evolved from **Prakrit languages**, particularly from **Paishachi Prakrit**, which was spoken in northern India. It transitioned to

Apabhraṃśa around the **7th century AD**, stabilizing by the **10th century**. Early Punjabi literature dates back to the **Nath Yogi-era** (9th to 14th century).

The language progressed through stages:

- **Old Punjabi**: 10th to 16th centuries.
- **Medieval Punjabi**: 16th to 19th centuries.

Arabic and Persian Influences:

The historical influence of **Arabic** and **Persian** began with the Muslim conquests in the Indian subcontinent. Punjabi absorbed many Persian and Arabic words, especially after the fall of the Sikh Empire when Urdu became the official language of Punjab.

Modern influences also include **Portuguese**, **Greek**, **Chagatai**, **Japanese**, **Chinese**, and **English**, but the primary influences remain Arabic and Persian.

Modern Times:

Modern Punjabi emerged in the **19th century** and has two main varieties:

- **Western Punjabi (Lahnda)**: Predominant in Pakistan.
- **Eastern Punjabi (Charda)**: Predominant in India.

The **Majhi dialect**, originating in the Majha region, serves as the standard for both education and mass media in India and Pakistan.

- **In India**: Gurmukhi is the official script for Punjabi, often written in Latin script informally due to English influence.
- **In Pakistan**: Shahmukhi is used, often closely resembling the Urdu alphabet but with some distinct characters to accommodate Punjabi phonology.

Geographic Distribution:

- **Pakistan**: Punjabi is the most widely spoken language.
- **India**: Official language of Punjab; additional official status in Haryana and Delhi.

- **Diaspora**: Significant populations in Canada (670,000 speakers), the UK (300,000), the US (280,000), and smaller communities elsewhere.

Major Dialects:

A. **Standard Punjabi (Majhi)**:
   - Central/Eastern Punjabi, widely used in media and education, particularly in Lahore and Amritsar.

B. **Eastern Punjabi**:
   - Predominantly spoken in Indian Punjab, includes dialects such as **Malwai**, **Doabi**, **Puadhi**, and the extinct **Lubanki**.

C. **Western Punjabi (Lahnda)**:
   - Includes various dialects spoken in western areas of Pakistani Punjab and parts of Azad Kashmir, such as **Saraiki**, **Pahari-Pothwari**, and **Hindko**. It also includes dialects grouped under **Jatki Punjabi** and the mixed **Khetrani** variety.

Punjabi, rich in history and diversity, reflects the cultural and linguistic evolution of the Punjab region. Its unique tonal qualities, extensive vocabulary influenced by various languages, and regional dialects highlight its importance as both a cultural heritage and a means of communication across borders.

Rajasthan:

Official Language: Hindi

Sikkim:

Official Language: English, Nepali, Sikkimese, Lepcha

Nepali:

A. **Classification**:

- Indo-Aryan language, part of the Eastern Pahari group of the Northern zone of Indo-Aryan languages.

B. **Geographic Distribution**:

- **Nepal**: Official language and widely spoken; approximately 44.6% of the population speaks it as their first language.
- **India**: Recognized in Sikkim and the Gorkhaland Territorial Administration in West Bengal; approximately 2.9 million speakers.
- **Bhutan**: Spoken by about 25% of the population; significant number of native speakers known as Lhotshampa.
- **Diaspora**: Spoken in countries like Australia, Myanmar, Brunei, and within Nepali communities globally.

C. **Historical Development**:

- Originated in the Sinja Valley of Karnali Province between the 10th and 14th centuries, evolving from Middle Indo-Aryan apabhraṃśa vernaculars.
- Institutionalized during the Gorkha Kingdom (16th century); significant literary development in the 19th century.
- Earliest known Nepali inscription dates back to the reign of King Bhupal Damupal around 981 AD.

D. **Linguistic Features**:

- **Syntax**: Primarily subject–object–verb (SOV) word order.
- **Honorifics**: Three levels (low, medium, high) based on respect.
- **Grammatical Structure**: Highly fusional with a simplified declensional system compared to older languages.

E. **Etymology**:
- The term "Nepali" derived from "Nepal," officially adopted in 1933.
- Previous names include "Khas Kura" (language of the Khas people) and "Gorakhā Bhāṣā" (language of the Gorkhas).

F. **Literary Development**:
- 19th century saw significant works, notably Bhanubhakta Acharya's translation of the Ramayana into Nepali, leading to cultural unification.
- Modern period began in the early 20th century, with attempts by the Rana dynasty to promote Nepali in education.

Related Languages in Sikkim:

A. **Sikkimese**:
- Also known as Bhutia or Drenjongké; belongs to the Tibeto-Burman language family.
- Official language of Sikkim, introduced as a written language in 1975.
- Written in Sambhota script and Zhang Yeshe De Script, influenced by Classical Tibetan.

B. **Lepcha**:
- An endangered Himalayish language spoken by the Lepcha people in Sikkim and parts of West Bengal and Bhutan.
- Despite preservation efforts, its use is declining, largely replaced by Nepali.
- Features its own indigenous script and is used in some educational contexts.

Cultural and Political Context:

A. **Official Status**:
- Nepali is the official language of Nepal and recognized in Indian states like Sikkim.

- Not officially recognized in Bhutan despite being spoken by a significant portion of the population.

B. **Language Movement**:

- In India, movements in the 1980s sought to include Nepali in the Eighth Schedule of the Constitution, leading to its official recognition in various regions.

C. **Cultural Significance**:

- Nepali serves as a symbol of national identity and cultural heritage, promoting unity among diverse ethnic groups within Nepal and the diaspora.

The Nepali language, with its rich history, diverse speakers, and ongoing evolution, remains a vital aspect of cultural identity in South Asia, influencing literature, education, and social cohesion.

Lepcha Language:

A. **Population and Distribution**:

- Spoken by minority communities in India (Sikkim, West Bengal), Nepal, and Bhutan.
- Considered an aboriginal language, predating Tibetan languages (e.g., Sikkimese, Dzongkha) and the Nepali language.
- Comprises four main communities:
    - **Renjóngmú** (Sikkim)
    - **Támsángmú** (Kalimpong, Kurseong, Mirik)
    - **Iilámmú** (Ilam District, Nepal)
    - **Promú** (Southwestern Bhutan)
- Indian census reported approximately 50,000 speakers, but estimates suggest around 30,000 native speakers in India.

B. **Classification**:

- Difficult to classify linguistically; suggested to be closest to Mahakiranti languages (Himalayish family).
- Internally diverse, influenced lexically by surrounding major languages.

- Possible Austroasiatic substratum from an extinct branch called "Rongic."

C. **Script and Romanization**:
- Written in the **Lepcha script** (róng), a syllabic script with unclear genealogy, initially influenced by Chinese writing.
- Early literary works used Tibetan script before the development of the Lepcha script.
- Romanization varies, with Mainwaring's system (1876) being the most prevalent; other linguists have used modifications based on European languages.

Additional Official Languages in the Region:

Gurung Language:

A. **Population and Distribution**:
- Known as Tamu Kyi or Tamu Bhāṣā, spoken by the Gurung people in Nepal, India, Bhutan, and the diaspora (e.g., Singapore, Hong Kong).
- Population figures: 227,918 in 1991; 325,622 in 2011 (Nepal).

B. **Geographical Distribution**:
- Spoken in Gandaki Province (Kaski, Syangja, Lamjung, Tanahu, Gorkha, Manang, Mustang) and Dhawalagiri Zone (Parbat District).
- Also found in South, West, and East Sikkim in India.

C. **Classification**:
- Part of the Tibeto-Burman family, classified within the Bodic division.
- Includes cognates that link it to languages like Tamang and Thakali.
- Contains dialectical variations and notable structural differences from Nepali.

Limbu Language:

A. Population and Distribution:

- Spoken by the Limbu people (Yakthung) in Nepal, Northeast India (Darjeeling, Kalimpong, Sikkim, Assam, Nagaland), and Bhutan.
- Four main dialects: Phedape, Chhathare, Tambarkhole, Panthare, with Phedape being widely understood.

B. Geographical Distribution:

- East of the Arun River, particularly in Koshi Province (Ilam, Dhankuta, Jhapa, Morang, Panchthar, Sankhuwasabha, Sunsari, Taplejung, Terhathum).

C. Official Status:

- Recognized as an official language in Province No. 1 in Nepal; used in local municipalities.
- In India, recognized as an additional official language in Sikkim, with a dedicated edition of the Sikkim Herald.

Magar Language:

A. Population and Distribution:

- Magar Dhut is spoken mainly in Nepal, southern Bhutan, and parts of India (Darjeeling, Sikkim).
- Approximately 810,000 speakers in Nepal.

B. Geographical Distribution:

- **Western Magar**: Palpa and Syangja districts in Nepal.
- **Eastern Magar**: Gorkha, Nawalparasi, Tanahu, and parts of eastern Nepal; scattered communities in India (Sikkim, Darjeeling, Assam, Manipur) and Bhutan.

C. Cultural Context:

- The government of Nepal has developed curricula for teaching the Magar language, though implementation in schools has been limited, often favouring Nepali.

- Two major dialect groups: Eastern and Western Magar, with significant structural differences leading to non-mutual intelligibility.

Lepcha is an aboriginal language with rich historical significance in the Himalayas, while **Gurung**, **Limbu**, and **Magar** represent important Sino-Tibetan languages of the region, each with distinct linguistic characteristics, cultural identities, and varying degrees of official recognition.

These languages play a crucial role in preserving the cultural heritage of their respective communities, fostering identity, and maintaining linguistic diversity in Nepal and neighbouring regions.

Sunwar Language:

A. **Classification**: A Kiranti language within the Sino-Tibetan family.

B. **Alternate Names**: Also called Sunuwar, Kõinch, Kõits Lo, Kiranti-Kõits, Mukhiya.

C. **Speakers**: Approximately 40,000 speakers, primarily located in eastern Nepal.

D. **Common Names**: Referred to as Koic by many ethnic Sunwar; speakers often have the surname Sunuvār.

E. **Geographic Distribution**:
   - Primarily spoken in villages along the Likhu Khola river in Okhaldhūngā and Rāmechāp Districts, Nepal.
   - Located about 1,800 meters above sea level in agricultural communities.

F. **Lifestyle**: Many households are farmers, growing crops and raising livestock; communities engage in local market trade.

G. **Climate**: Experiences cold winters and heavy monsoon rainfall from June to August, with freezing temperatures in winter but no snowfall.

Newari Language:

A. **Classification**: A Sino-Tibetan language, officially known as Nepal Bhasa in Nepal.

B. **Historical Significance**: Was the administrative language from the 14th to late 18th century.

C. **Current Status**: Classified as "definitely endangered" by UNESCO due to a decline in speakers from 75% in 1952 to 44% by 1991.

D. **Names**: "Nepal Bhasa" means "Nepalese language"; "Newari" is considered derogatory.

E. **Geographic Distribution**:
   - Spoken by over a million people, mainly in the Kathmandu Valley and surrounding regions.
   - Presence in Dolakha, Banepa, and some regions in India (West Bengal & Sikkim) and Tibet.
   - Growing diaspora due to emigration to countries like the US, UK, Australia, and Japan.

F. **Official Status**:
   - Recognized as an official language in several municipalities in Nepal; efforts are ongoing to promote its status in various provinces.
   - In Sikkim, it is an additional official language for cultural preservation.

G. **Education**: Included in school curriculums; higher education offered at Tribhuvan University and language classes available in some municipalities.

H. **Historical Development**:
   - Evolved through significant contact with Indo-European languages, particularly Sanskrit.
   - Early references to the language date back to the 14th century.

I. **Literary Tradition**: Flourished during the Malla period; faced suppression during the Rana regime.

Classification Challenges: The precise placement of Newar within the Tibeto-Burman family is debated; influenced by mixed linguistic heritage and historical separation from other languages.

Historical Development:

- **Divergence and Vocabulary**: Newari and Chepang language diverged around 2200 BC. Newari shares approximately 28% of its vocabulary with Chepang and over 50% of its vocabulary is derived from Indo-European languages, influenced by Sanskrit, Maithili, Persian, Urdu, Hindi, and Nepali.
- **Early Records**: The earliest known written records of Newar appeared in Sanskrit inscriptions from the fifth century. By the 12th century, Newar was recorded in inscriptions, with significant works such as the **Gopalarajavamsavali** emerging in the 14th century.
- **Court Language**: From the 14th to the late 18th centuries, Newar served as the court and administrative language of Nepal, documented in stone and copper inscriptions, official decrees, and literary works.

Literature and Cultural Significance:

- **Classical Period (1505–1847)**: A golden age for Newar literature with prolific output in poetry, stories, and dramas, largely driven by royal patronage. Notable figures included Mahindra Malla and Siddhi Narsingh Malla.
- **Decline**: The language began to decline post-18th century with the Gorkha conquest, which replaced Newar with the Gorkhali language in official settings. Under the Rana regime, strict suppression of Newar occurred, including bans on literature and legal documentation.
- **Renaissance Era (1909–1941)**: A resurgence in literary activity occurred, led by figures such as Nisthananda Bajracharya and Siddhidas Mahaju, despite official

disapproval. This period saw the publication of grammar texts and the first printed books in Newar.

Struggles for Recognition:

- **Nepal Bhasha Movement**: The movement for linguistic rights emerged against oppressive policies from the Shah dynasty through the Rana regime. Activists fought for the preservation of Newar and faced significant pushback, including imprisonment.
- **Post-1990 Developments**: The 1990 People's Movement allowed for greater freedom for Newar, resulting in recognition of Nepal as a multilingual country. Despite this, official recognition of Newar in public administration faced legal challenges.
- **Ongoing Challenges**: Even after the 2006 People's Movement and the establishment of a republic, practical use of Newar in governance remains limited, with ongoing efforts for its development through education and media.

Literature Forms:

- **Drama**: Traditional dramas, often based on deities and morality, play a vital role in Newar culture. They are performed at designated times in the Nepal Sambat calendar.
- **Poetry**: Newar poetry flourished during the Malla dynasty, with many rulers being celebrated poets.
- **Prose Fiction**: This genre is relatively new, with most earlier literature in poetic form. Recent years have seen a rise in collections of short stories.
- **Storytelling**: Verbal storytelling remains significant in Newar culture, with tales reflecting the valley's history and norms. Increasing literacy has led to the documentation of these stories.

External Influence:

- **Inscriptions Beyond the Valley**: Newar inscriptions are found beyond the Kathmandu Valley, including significant examples in Gorkha and Tibet, showcasing the language's historical reach and trade connections.

Newar has a rich historical and cultural tapestry, marked by periods of flourishing creativity and significant challenges to its survival. The ongoing efforts to revitalize and recognize Newar reflect its importance in the cultural identity of the Newar people and Nepal as a whole.

Dialects:

Newar Dialect Clusters:

A. Kansakar's Classification:

- **Western Dialects:**
  - ♦ Includes areas like Tansen (Palpa), Butwal, Nepalgunj, Old Pokhara, Dumre, Bandipur, Ridhi (Gulmi), Baglung, and Dotili/Silgadi.
- **Central Dialects:**
  - ♦ Encompasses Kathmandu, Lalitpur, Bhaktapur, Thimi, Kirtipur, and several others, including various localities in Kavrepalanchok District.
- **Eastern Dialects:**
  - ♦ Covers regions such as Chainpur, Dharan, Dolakha, Sindhupalchok, and extends to areas like Taplejung and Jhapa.

B. Kapali's Mutual Intelligibility Classification:

- **Nepa Valley (Kathmandu Valley):**
  - ♦ Divided into Eastern (Bhaktapur and adjacent areas) and Western (Kathmandu and Lalitpur).

- **Dwalkha:**
  - Encompasses Dolakha and parts of Sindhupalchok and Kavre districts.
- **Smaller Dialects:**
  - Includes variations based on locality (like Pyang gaan) and caste groups (like Gopali, Balami, and Pahari).

Specific Dialects and Their Characteristics:

- **Bhaktapur (Khwapey Bhāy):**
  - Considered more archaic with variations in language use in Bhaktapur, Banepa, Panauti, and Dhulikhel.
- **Chitlang:**
  - Predominantly spoken in Chitlang, south of the Kathmandu Valley, known for its strong Balami caste presence.
- **Dolakha:**
  - This dialect retains many archaic features and is seen as a well-preserved form of Newar.
- **Kathmandu-Lalitpur:**
  - **Kathmandu Dialect (Yenmi Bhāy):** Dominant and close to the standard academic form.
  - **Lalitpur Dialect (Yeley Bhāy):** Also widely used and forms the basis for most Nepal Bhasa publications.
- **Pahari:**
  - A variation spoken by the Pahari caste, often distinguished by specific vocabulary.
- **Pyangaan:**
  - Unique to the town of Pyangaan in Lalitpur district.

Dialectical Diversity and Religion:

Religious affiliations have contributed to subtle dialectical variations, particularly between Newar Hindus and Buddhists.

Certain vocabulary may differ, although the dialects of Kathmandu and Patan remain similar. The influence of other religions, such as Christianity and Islam, has also introduced new linguistic elements.

External Languages:

A. Kiranti Languages:

- A significant family of Sino-Tibetan languages spoken mainly by the Kirati people in Nepal and parts of India.
- Key languages include Limbu, Sunuwar, Bantawa, and several others, characterized by complex verb structures.

B. Sherpa Language:

- A Tibetic language spoken by the Sherpa community, mainly in the Khumbu region of Nepal and parts of Sikkim and Tibet. It has a subject-object-verb (SOV) structure and is predominantly oral.

C. Tamang Language:

- A dialect cluster referred to as Tamang, which includes various regional forms spoken in Nepal and surrounding areas. Eastern Tamang is the most prominent, showing significant lexical similarity to other Tamang languages.

The linguistic landscape of the Newar community is rich and diverse, influenced by historical developments, geographical distinctions, and cultural dynamics. This complexity is mirrored in the relationships and mutual intelligibility among Newar dialects and their connections to external languages like Kiranti, Sherpa, and Tamang.

The Tamang language is indeed a significant component of the Sino-Tibetan language family, primarily spoken in Nepal. Here's a detailed overview of its dialects, sub-dialects, and geographical distribution:

Tamang Dialects and Sub-Dialects

A. Eastern Tamang

- **Population:** Approximately 759,000 in Nepal (2000 WCD), with a total population of about 773,000 across all countries.
- **Sub-Dialects:**
    - **Outer-Eastern Tamang (Sailung Tamang)**
    - **Central-Eastern Tamang (Temal Tamang)**
    - **Southwestern Tamang:** Includes various local variants such as:
    - Kath-Bhotiya
    - Lama Bhote
    - Murmi
    - Rongba
    - Sain
    - Tamang Gyoi
    - Tamang Gyot
    - Tamang Lengmo
    - Tamang Tam

B. Western Tamang

- **Population:** Approximately 323,000 (2000 WCD).
- **Sub-Dialects:**
    - **Trisuli:** Spoken in Nuwakot.
    - **Rasuwa:** A dialect from the Rasuwa district.
    - **Northwestern dialect (Dhading):** Previously had a separate ISO code (tmk), merged with tdg in 2023. Population was about 55,000 (1991 census), primarily spoken in the central mountainous area of Nuwakot District, Bagmati Province.
    - **Southwestern dialect of Western Tamang:** Specific characteristics of this dialect are not detailed.

C. Eastern Gorkha Tamang

- **Population:** Approximately 4,000 (2000 WCD).
- **Sub-Dialects:**
    - **Kasigaon**
    - **Kerounja**

Geographical Distribution of Tamang Language Varieties:

Eastern Tamang:

- **Bagmati Province:**
    - Bhaktapur District
    - Chitwan District
    - Dolkha District
    - Kathmandu District
    - Kavrepalanchok District
    - Lalitpur District
    - Makwanpur District
    - Eastern Nuwakot District
    - Ramechhap District
    - Sindhuli District
    - Western Sindhupalchowk District
- **Province No. 1:**
    - Okhaldhunga District
    - Western Khotang District
    - Udayapur District

South western Tamang:

- **Bagmati Province:**
    - Chitwan District
    - Southern Dhading District
    - Northwestern areas of Kathmandu District
    - Northwestern Makwanpur District

- **Province No. 2:**
    - Bara District
    - Parsa District
    - Rautahat District

Western Tamang:

- **Bagmati Province:**
    - Western Nuwakot District
    - Rasuwa District
    - Dhading District
    - Northwestern Makwanpur District (including Phakel, Chakhel, Khulekhani, Markhu, Tistung, and Palung)
    - Northern Kathmandu District (including Jhor, Thoka, and Gagal Phedi)
    - Northeastern Sindhupalchok District (areas like Bhote Namlan and Bhote Chaur near the Trishuli River toward the Budhi Gandaki River)

The Tamang language's rich dialectal diversity is not only a reflection of its broad geographic distribution across various provinces in Nepal but also highlights the unique cultural identities of the Tamang-speaking communities. Each dialect and sub-dialect carries its distinct characteristics, shaped by historical, social, and environmental influences. As the most widely spoken Sino-Tibetan language in Nepal, Tamang plays a vital role in the linguistic and cultural landscape of the region.

Tamilnadu:

Official Language: Tamil

Tamil is a rich and ancient language, integral to the cultural identity of the Tamil people and with a long and storied history. Here's a summary of key points regarding its classification, historical development, cultural significance, and modern usage:

Overview of Tamil:

- **Language Family:** Tamil is a Dravidian language, part of a larger family of around 26 languages native to South Asia. It has a close relationship with Malayalam, having diverged around the 9th century AD.
- **Official Status:** Tamil is the official language of Tamil Nadu and the union territory of Puducherry in India, as well as an official language in Sri Lanka and Singapore.
- **Global Presence:** It is spoken by Tamil communities worldwide, including significant populations in Malaysia, Myanmar, South Africa, the United Kingdom, the United States, Canada, Australia, New Zealand, and the Gulf countries.

Historical Significance:

- **Classical Status:** Tamil was the first Indian language to be designated as a classical language and is one of the longest-surviving classical languages in the world, with a continuous literary tradition dating back over 2,000 years.
- **Early Literature:** The oldest records of Tamil literature, known as Sangam literature, date from approximately 300 BC to AD 300. The Tolkāppiyam, a seminal work on Tamil grammar, is among the earliest texts from this period.
- **Archaeological Evidence:** Tamil inscriptions, such as those written in Tamil-Brahmi script, have been found in India, Sri Lanka, and even trade artifacts in Egypt and Thailand, indicating its historical significance as a language of trade and culture.

Language Development:

- **Periods of Tamil:**
  - **Old Tamil (300 BC – AD 700):** Characterized by inscriptions and early literary works, it was primarily written in Tamil-Brahmi script.

  - **Middle Tamil (700 – 1600):** This period saw significant phonological and grammatical changes, including the emergence of the present tense.
  - **Modern Tamil (1600 – present):** The Nannūl serves as a standard for modern literary Tamil, while spoken Tamil has evolved with numerous changes influenced by European languages.
- Cultural Importance:
  - **Literary Tradition:** The variety and quality of classical Tamil literature have earned it recognition as one of the great classical traditions in the world. The language boasts a diverse corpus of poetry, philosophy, and religious texts.
  - **Religious and Mythological Context:** In Hindu mythology, Tamil is personified as "Tamil Thāi" (Mother Tamil), and is said to have been brought to the people by Lord Shiva, along with sage Agastya.
  - **Etymology:** The name "Tamil" may derive from "tam-miḻ," meaning "self-speak" or "our own speech," reflecting the language's deep cultural roots.

Modern Usage and Evolution:

- **Print and Media:** The first Tamil book was published in 1578, and today Tamil has a vibrant media presence with numerous newspapers and magazines, showcasing the language's ongoing relevance.
- **Influence of Other Languages:** Contact with European languages has led to changes in written and spoken Tamil, including the adoption of new punctuation and syntax, while a movement towards linguistic purism has sought to minimize Sanskrit influences.

Tamil is a dynamic and evolving language that reflects the history, culture, and identity of the Tamil people. Its extensive literary tradition, ancient roots, and contemporary relevance continue to shape its role in South Asia and beyond.

Tamil's geographic distribution, legal status, and dialectical diversity contribute significantly to its cultural richness and historical significance. Here's a detailed overview of these aspects:

Geographic Distribution:

A. Primary Regions:

- **India:** Tamil is the primary language in Tamil Nadu and Puducherry. Historically, it was the major language of administration and literature in parts of Kerala and southern Andhra Pradesh until the 12th century.
- **Sri Lanka:** Tamil is widely spoken in the Northern and Eastern provinces, with significant populations in urban areas like Colombo.

B. Minority Groups:

- Tamil is spoken by minority groups in various Indian states, including Karnataka, Telangana, Andhra Pradesh, Kerala, Maharashtra, Gujarat, Delhi, and the Andaman and Nicobar Islands.

C. Global Tamil Diaspora:

- Significant Tamil-speaking populations exist in countries like Malaysia, Singapore, the Philippines, Mauritius, South Africa, Indonesia, Thailand, and Vietnam, primarily as descendants of colonial-era migrants.
- In Malaysia, Tamil is a medium of instruction in government schools, and in Canada, it is taught in local school boards and universities. Tamil Heritage Month is celebrated in January.

D. Other Regions:

- Tamil-speaking communities also exist in Pakistan (Karachi), Réunion, Guyana, Fiji, Suriname, and Trinidad and Tobago, though fluency varies.

Legal Status:

- **Official Language Recognition:**
    - ♦ Tamil is an official language of Tamil Nadu, Puducherry, and the Andaman and Nicobar Islands in India. It holds national language status in Sri Lanka alongside Sinhala and is an official language in Singapore.
    - ♦ In Malaysia, there are Tamil medium schools, and in South Africa, it enjoys protection under the Constitution, with education offered in Tamil in KwaZulu-Natal.
- **Classical Language Status:**
    - ♦ In 2004, Tamil was recognized as the first classical language of India, a significant achievement that underscores its historical and cultural importance.

Dialects:

A. **Regional Variations:**
- ♦ Tamil dialects exhibit significant phonological changes and sound shifts. For example, the word for "here" varies across dialects, showcasing differences in pronunciation.
- ♦ Major dialects include Central Tamil, Kongu Tamil, Madras Bashai, Madurai Tamil, and regional variations in Sri Lanka like Batticaloa and Jaffna Tamil.

B. **Influences and Loanwords:**
- ♦ Some dialects, like those in Palakkad and Kanyakumari, are influenced by Malayalam, incorporating loanwords and distinct phonetic styles.
- ♦ In Sri Lanka, Tamil dialects have absorbed loanwords from Portuguese, Dutch, and English.

C. **Sociolects and Caste Variations:**
- ♦ Caste-specific sociolects exist, with Tamil Brahmins exhibiting unique phonetic features and a higher presence of Sanskrit loanwords.

D. **Literary and Spoken Forms:**

- Tamil encompasses various forms:
  - **Sankattamil̲:** Classical literary style.
  - **Centamil̲:** Modern literary style used in formal contexts.
  - **Koṭuntamil̲:** Colloquial form gaining popularity in media and everyday speech.
- The distinction between these forms contributes to a stylistic continuum where elements from one can be used in another context.

E. **Standardization:**

- Standard spoken Tamil in India has been influenced by Thanjavur and Madurai dialects, while in Sri Lanka, the Jaffna dialect serves as the basis for the standard.

The geographic spread, legal recognition, and rich tapestry of dialects highlight Tamil's unique position as a language that is not only deeply rooted in the history and culture of its native speakers but also vibrant and evolving in contemporary contexts. Its classical status and global presence further underscore its significance as a living language with a diverse and dynamic heritage.

Additional Officail Language: English

Telangana:

Official Language: Telugu

Telugu, a Dravidian language, is primarily spoken in Andhra Pradesh and Telangana, where it holds official status, and by about 96 million people worldwide. Recognized as one of India's twenty-two scheduled languages and one of six classical languages, it is the most widely spoken Dravidian tongue and ranks as the 14th most spoken native language globally. Telugu's modern standard form stems from dialects of Coastal Andhra and Rayalaseema. It has a rich history, with inscriptions dating back to 575 CE and a literary tradition spanning over a millennium. Telugu was a cultural and bureaucratic language under various South Indian dynasties and influenced Carnatic music, where its mellifluous quality is celebrated. Historically called "Telugu" or "Tenugu," its etymology ties to Proto-Dravidian roots. While early grammarians like Atharvana Acharya and Appa Kavi contributed to its linguistic understanding, scholars debate its derivation from "Trilinga," considering alternate Sanskritized origins. Telugu's global footprint extends to the diaspora and regions like the United States, where it is the fastest-growing language.

- **Language Family & Official Status**:
- Telugu is a Dravidian language spoken mainly in Andhra Pradesh and Telangana, India.
- It is the official language in these states and one of India's 22 scheduled languages.
- Recognized as a classical language of India.
- **Demographics**:
- Spoken by ~96 million people, making it the most widely spoken Dravidian language.
- Ranked as the 14th most spoken native language in the world.
- **Geographical Spread**:
- Spoken in Indian states like Karnataka, Tamil Nadu, Maharashtra, Chhattisgarh, Odisha, and union territories such as Puducherry and Andaman & Nicobar Islands.
- Significant diaspora presence in countries like the US, Canada, Australia, UAE, and South Africa.
- **Cultural Significance**:
- Known for its musical quality, widely used in Carnatic music.
- Celebrated as a language of high culture in South India, similar to French in Europe during the precolonial era.
- **Historical Roots**:
- Proto-Telugu emerged around 1000 BCE, with the earliest inscriptions from 575 CE.

- Was the court language of South Indian dynasties like the Eastern Chalukyas, Kakatiyas, and Vijayanagara Empire.
- **Literary Contributions**:
- Over 1,000 years of continuous literary tradition, with notable works like Pavuluri Mallana's *Sāra Sangraha Ganitamu* (11th century).
- Features unique literary forms like *Avadhānaṃ*.
- **Etymology**:
- Evolved from "Tenuṅgu" (south) in Proto-Dravidian, with debated links to "Trilinga."
- Modern scholarly consensus leans towards Telugu being the older term.
- **Global Recognition**:
- Fastest-growing language in the US.
- Protected in South Africa, offered as an optional third language in KwaZulu-Natal schools.

History:

1. Historical and Linguistic Evolution

- Telugu descends from Proto-Dravidian, spoken ~4th millennium BCE.
- Proto-Telugu split from Proto South-Central Dravidian ~1000 BCE.
- Linguistic phases:
  - Proto-Telugu (≤1000 BCE) → Pre-historic Telugu (600 BCE–200 BCE) → Old Telugu (200 BCE–1000 CE) → Middle Telugu (1000 CE–1600 CE) → Modern Telugu (1600 CE–Present).
- Identified as one of the most conservative Dravidian languages.

2. Early Records

- First word in Telugu: *Nāgabu* (2nd century BCE) found in Amaravati Stupa.
- Telugu inscriptions date to ~575 CE, attributed to Renati Choda king Dhanunjaya.
- Telugu was used in Satavahana, Vishnukundina, and Andhra Ikshvaku inscriptions.

3. Linguistic Features

- Retained phonemes like retroflex approximants (/ɻ/) and voiced alveolar plosives (/d/).
- Past vs. non-past tenses and masculine vs. non-masculine genders in early Telugu.
- Significant phonetic and grammatical evolution over centuries.

4. Influence of Sanskrit and Persian

- Heavily influenced by Sanskrit and Prakrit during early literary periods.
- Persian and Arabic influences seen in Hyderabad region under Sultanates and Nizams.

5. Literary and Cultural Milestones

- Telugu literature flourished during the Vijayanagara Empire (1336–17th century).
- Golden Age under Krishnadevaraya (16th century).
- Known as the "Italian of the East" for its vowel-ending words (noted by Niccolò de' Conti).

6. Geographic and Global Spread

- Native to Andhra Pradesh, Telangana, and Yanam (Puducherry).
- Significant populations in Karnataka, Tamil Nadu, Maharashtra, Odisha, and abroad in the US, Canada, UAE, Australia, and South Africa.

- Fastest-growing language in the US (86% growth from 2010–2017).

7. Legal Status and Recognition

- Official language in Andhra Pradesh, Telangana, and Yanam.
- Classified as a classical language of India.
- Protected language in South Africa, taught as a subject in schools.

8. Epigraphical Records

- Over 14,000 Telugu inscriptions exist, making it one of the most densely inscribed languages.
- Found in Andhra Pradesh, Telangana, Karnataka, Tamil Nadu, Odisha, and even in Myanmar and Indonesia.

9. Modern Developments

- Standardized form popularized through mass media like films, TV, and newspapers.
- Fourth most spoken Indian language and widely respected for its literary and cultural heritage.
- Telugu Language Day celebrated annually on August 29.

Geographical Influences:

Telugu Region Boundaries, Place Names, and Dialects:

1. Region Boundaries

- **Historical Boundaries:**
  - **North:** Mahendra Mountain in modern Ganjam district, Odisha.
  - **South:** Srikalahasteeswara Temple in Tirupati district.
  - **West:** Srisailam in Nandyal district.
- **16th Century Boundaries:**
  - **North:** Simhachalam (present-day Visakhapatnam).
  - **South:** Tirumala (Chittoor district).

2. Telugu Place Names

- **Common suffixes in Telugu place names include:**
    - *-ooru, -pudi, -padu, -peta, -pattanam, -wada, -cherla, -gudem, -konda, -palem, -pakam,* etc.
- **Examples:**
    - **Andhra Pradesh:** Nellore, Tadepalligudem, Vijayawada, Guntur, Sattenapalle, Vizianagaram.
    - **Telangana:** Warangal, Siddipet, Mancherial, Peddapalli, Miryalaguda.

3. Dialects of Telugu

- **Four Regional Dialects:**
    - **Northern:** Telangana
    - **Southern:** Rayalaseema
    - **Central:** Coastal Andhra
    - **Eastern:** North Andhra
- **Colloquial Grouping:** Telangana, Rayalaseema, and Coastal Andhra dialects.
- **Closely Related Languages/Dialects:**
    - Waddar, Chenchu, Manna-Dora.
- **Additional Dialects:**
    - Berad, Dasari, Dommara, Golari, Kamathi, Komtao, Konda-Reddi, Salewari, Vadaga, Srikakula, Visakhapatnam, East Godavari, Nellore, Guntur, Vadari Bangalore, and Yanadi.

Additional Official Language: Urdu

Tripura:

Official Language: Bengali, English, Kokborok

Bengali:

1. General Facts

- **Name:** Bengali (endonym: Bangla)
- **Language Family:** Indo-Aryan
- **Native Region:** Bengal (Bangladesh and West Bengal, India)
- **Speakers (2021):**
    - **Native:** ~240 million
    - **Total:** ~281 million
- **Global Rank:**
    - 6th most spoken native language
    - 7th most spoken overall
- **Official Status:**
    - Bangladesh (national and sole official language)
    - Indian states: West Bengal, Tripura, Barak Valley (Assam), and Jharkhand (second official language).

2. Historical Development

- **Ancient Period:**
    - Rooted in *Magadhi Prakrit* and influenced by Sanskrit during the Gupta Empire.
    - Transitioned through *Ardha Magadhi* and *Apabhraṃśa.*
- **Medieval Period:**
    - *Middle Bengali* (1400–1800) emerged.
    - Influenced by Arabic, Persian, and Turkic languages due to Islamic cultural exchanges.
    - Major literary works: *Yusuf-Zulekha* and *Srikrishna Kirtana.*
- **Modern Period:**
    - Standardized in the 19th–20th centuries based on the West-Central (Nadia) dialect.
    - Influenced by Sanskrit, Pali, Persian, Arabic, and Austroasiatic languages.

3. Role in History and Culture

- **Bengali Renaissance:** Rich literary development in the 19th century.
- **Language Movement (1948–1956):**
  - Protest for Bengali's recognition in Pakistan.
  - 21 February 1952: Five martyrs died defending the language.
  - Led to the creation of Bangladesh (1971).
  - UNESCO declared 21 February *International Mother Language Day* (1999).
- **UN Language Status:** Adopted as an unofficial language (2022).

4. Geographical Distribution

- **Primary Region:**
  - Bangladesh (98% of the population).
  - Indian states: West Bengal, Tripura, Assam, Jharkhand.
- **Diaspora:** Significant presence in Europe, the U.S., Middle East, Singapore, Malaysia, and Australia.

5. Dialects

- **Main Clusters (by Suniti Kumar Chatterji):**
  - *Rarhi, Vangiya, Kamrupi, Varendri.*
- **Notable Dialects:**
  - Southwestern (basis for Standard Colloquial Bengali).
  - Eastern (e.g., Sylheti, Chittagonian).
  - Other regional varieties: Barendri, Rangpuriya, Jashore, Dhakiya, Barisal, etc.
- **Diglossia:**
  - **Sadhu Bhasha:** Formal, archaic style (used in older literature).
  - **Chôlito Bhasha:** Modern standard colloquial style.

6. Literary and Cultural Contributions

- National anthems of Bangladesh (*Amar Sonar Bangla*) and India (*Jana Gana Mana*) written in Bengali.
- *Vande Mataram* and *Notuner Gaan* (Bangladesh's national march) are Bengali compositions.
- **Literary figures:** Rabindranath Tagore, Kazi Nazrul Islam, Bankim Chandra Chatterjee.

7. Key Features and Linguistic Influence

- Exhibits influence from Sanskrit, Pali, Persian, Arabic, and Austroasiatic languages.
- Features significant phonological variations, particularly between eastern and western dialects.
- Diglossic nature allows flexibility between formal and colloquial use.

8. Recognition and Future Prospects

- Proposals to make Bengali an official UN language remain under consideration.
- Continues to grow rapidly, with increasing prominence in global cultural and linguistic spheres.

Kokborok Language:

Kokborok (or Tripuri) is a Tibeto-Burman language of the Indian state of Tripura and neighbouring areas of Bangladesh.

Etymology:

- The term *Kokborok* is derived from *kok* meaning "verbal" or "language" and *borok* meaning "people" or "human."

Historical Background:

- Formerly known as *Tripuri* or *Tipra Kok*, the language name was officially changed in the 20th century.
- The language is tied to the heritage of the *Twipra* kingdom and the ethnic identity of its speakers.

- Kokborok has been documented since the 1st century AD, starting with the historical chronicles of the Tripuri kings.
- The original script, *Koloma*, was used for writing Kokborok, and the royal chronicle *Rajratnakar* was initially composed in Kokborok before being translated into Sanskrit and later into Bengali in the 19th century.
- During the 19th and 20th centuries, Kokborok was marginalized under the Tripuri monarchy, used mainly as a colloquial language.
- In 1979, Kokborok was declared an official language of Tripura. Since then, it has been integrated into the education system, starting at the primary level and now extending to postgraduate studies at Tripura University.

Modern Developments:

- Kokborok is taught from primary to postgraduate levels in Tripura.
- A certificate course was introduced in 1994, followed by a postgraduate diploma in 2001, and degree-level courses began in 2012.
- Master's degree programs in Kokborok were initiated in 2015 at Tripura University.
- Efforts are ongoing to recognize Kokborok as one of the official languages of India under the 8th Schedule of the Constitution.
- The official standard dialect is based on the variety spoken in Agartala, Tripura's capital.

Classification and Related Languages:

- Kokborok belongs to the Sino-Tibetan language family, specifically the Bodo–Garo branch.
- It shares linguistic ties with Bodo and Dimasa in Assam and Garo in Meghalaya and parts of Bangladesh.

Dialects:

- Kokborok consists of several dialects:
  - Usoi (Kau Brung)
  - Riang (Kau Bru)
  - Khagrachari (or "Trippera")
  - Mukchak (Barbakpur)
- Khagrachari displays the greatest dialectical diversity, with Naitong and Dendak varieties being used for literature.
- Some Tripuri clans' languages remain under-researched.

Linguistic Status and Recognition:

- The movement for inclusion in the 8th Schedule of the Indian Constitution reflects its growing cultural and linguistic significance.
- Efforts are focused on promoting the language's use in administrative, educational, and cultural contexts to preserve and enhance its status.

Uttar Pradesh:

Official Language: Hindi

Additional Official Language: Urdu

Uttarakhand:

Official Language: Hindi

Additional Official Language: Sanskrit

West Bengal:

Official Language: Bengali, English

Additional Official Languages: Nepali in Darjeeling and Kurseong Sub Divisions; Urdu, Hindi, Odia, Santali, Punjabi, Kamtapuri,

Rajbanshi, Kudmali/Kurmali, Kurukh and Telugu in Blocks, divisions or districts with population greater than 10 percent.

Languages of Union Terriotary in India

Union Terriotary	Official Language	Additional Official Language
Andaman and Nicobar Islands	Hindi, English	--
Dadra and Nagar Haveli and Daman and Diu	Hindi, English	Gujarati
Delhi	Hindi, English	Urdu, Punjabi
Ladakh	Hindi, English	--
Chandigarh	English	--
Lakshadweep	English	Malyalam
Jammu and Kashmir	Kashmiri, Dogri, Hindi, Urdu, English	--
Puducherry	Tamil, Telugu, Malyalam	English, French

Languages of Pakistan

A Multilingual Landscape:

Pakistan is home to a diverse array of languages, reflecting its rich cultural and ethnic mosaic. Over 70 languages are spoken as first languages, with significant linguistic diversity across its provinces and regions.

Language Groups:

Most languages spoken in Pakistan belong to the Indo-Iranian branch of the Indo-European language family, although there are notable exceptions.

National and Official Languages:

- **Urdu:** The national language and lingua franca, used for communication across Pakistan's diverse ethnic groups. While Urdu is spoken as a first language by only about 7% of the population, it holds immense symbolic and practical importance as a unifying language.

- **English:** Shares official status with Urdu and is widely used in government, legal proceedings, education, and business sectors.

Regional Languages with Over a Million Speakers:

1. **Punjabi:**
   - Spoken by over 40% of the population.
   - Predominantly in Punjab province.
2. **Pashto:**
   - Spoken in Khyber Pakhtunkhwa and parts of Balochistan.
   - Also spoken by Pashtun communities in urban areas.
3. **Sindhi:**
   - Primarily spoken in Sindh province.
   - Known for its literary and cultural contributions.
4. **Saraiki:**
   - Spoken in southern Punjab.
   - Closely related to Punjabi but regarded as a distinct language by its speakers.
5. **Balochi:**
   - Predominantly spoken in Balochistan.
   - Part of the Iranian branch of Indo-Iranian languages.
6. **Hindko:**
   - Spoken in Hazara Division of Khyber Pakhtunkhwa and parts of northern Punjab.
7. **Pahari-Pothwari:**
   - Spoken in the Potohar Plateau and parts of Azad Jammu and Kashmir.
8. **Brahui:**
   - A Dravidian language spoken in Balochistan, unique as a non-Indo-Iranian language.

Languages with Fewer than a Million Speakers:

There are around 60 such languages, including:

- Shina and Burushaski (spoken in Gilgit-Baltistan).
- Khowar (spoken in Chitral).
- Balti (a Tibetic language in Gilgit-Baltistan).
- Smaller languages in the Kalash valleys, such as Kalasha.

Linguistic Diversity and Challenges:

The linguistic landscape of Pakistan is marked by:

- **Multilingualism:** Many Pakistanis are bilingual or multilingual, often speaking a regional language alongside Urdu and/or English.
- **Language Preservation:** Efforts are needed to document and preserve the country's endangered languages, particularly those spoken by small communities.

Significance of Urdu as a Lingua Franca:

Despite being a second language for most, Urdu facilitates communication across Pakistan's ethnically and linguistically diverse population. Its role as a medium of instruction and cultural expression reinforces its status as a key component of national identity.

Linguistic Classification of Pakistan's Languages:

Pakistan's linguistic diversity encompasses several branches of the **Indo-European family** as well as languages outside of it. Below is a detailed classification of these languages:

1. Indo-Iranian Branch (Indo-European Family):

The majority of Pakistan's languages belong to the **Indo-Iranian branch**, which descends from Proto-Indo-Iranian, a language spoken around the late 3rd millennium BCE.

A. Indo-Aryan Subgroup:

Languages in eastern Pakistan primarily belong to this subgroup. They evolved from Old Indo-Aryan (e.g., Vedic Sanskrit) via Middle Indo-Aryan (Prakrits).

- **Lahnda Dialect Continuum**
  - ♦ **Saraiki**: ~26 million speakers, concentrated in southern Punjab.
  - ♦ **Hindko**: ~5 million speakers, spoken in Hazara (Khyber Pakhtunkhwa) and northern Punjab.
  - ♦ **Pahari/Pothwari**: ~3.5 million speakers, found in Pothohar (northern Punjab), Azad Jammu & Kashmir, and parts of Indian-administered Jammu & Kashmir.
  - ♦ **Khetrani**: ~20,000 speakers, spoken in northern Balochistan.
  - ♦ **Inku**: A possibly extinct language of Afghanistan.

B. Iranian Subgroup:

Languages spoken in western Pakistan predominantly belong to this subgroup, with strong roots in the Iranian Plateau.

- **Balochi Dialect Continuum:**
  - ♦ **Eastern Balochi**: Found in Balochistan and Sindh.
  - ♦ **Western Balochi**: Spoken in Iran and Afghanistan.
  - ♦ **Southern Balochi**: Found in southern Pakistan and nearby regions.
- **Pashto Dialect Continuum:**
  - ♦ **Northern Pashto**: Spoken in parts of Khyber Pakhtunkhwa.
  - ♦ **Central Pashto**: Widely spoken in Peshawar and adjacent areas.
  - ♦ **Southern Pashto**: Found in southern Khyber Pakhtunkhwa and northern Balochistan.

2. Languages Outside the Indo-European Family:

A. Dravidian Family:

- **Brahui**:
  - Spoken in central Balochistan, it is a **Dravidian language**, distinct from the predominantly Iranian linguistic environment around it.
  - Though it has Dravidian roots, much of its vocabulary is influenced by Balochi.

B. Tibeto-Burman Family:

- **Balti**:
  - A dialect of Ladakhi, belonging to the **Tibeto-Burman subgroup**.
  - Spoken in southern Gilgit–Baltistan and heavily influenced by Urdu and Persian.

C. Language Isolate:

- **Burushaski**:
  - A unique language with no proven relation to any linguistic family.
  - Spoken in the Hunza, Nagar, Yasin, and Ishkoman valleys of Gilgit–Baltistan.
  - Uses the Urdu script for written communication.

Linguistic Distribution and Influences:

- **Geographical Distribution**:
  - **Indo-Aryan languages** dominate the **eastern regions** (Punjab, Sindh).
  - **Iranian languages** are spoken in the **western regions** (Balochistan, Khyber Pakhtunkhwa).
  - Isolated languages such as **Burushaski** and **Balti** are found in the northern regions (Gilgit–Baltistan).

- **Cultural and Lexical Influences**:
  - Brahui has absorbed significant Balochi vocabulary.
  - Balti is influenced by Persian and Urdu, reflecting its historical and cultural exchanges.

List of Languages in Pakistan:

Pakistan is home to a diverse linguistic landscape, with a wide array of languages spoken across the country. According to the 2022 edition of *Ethnologue*, there are 77 established languages in Pakistan, of which 68 are indigenous and 9 are non-indigenous. These languages vary greatly in terms of the number of speakers, their vitality, and their geographical distribution. Below is a snapshot of some of the languages, highlighting their status and key features:

1. Aer Language:

- **Family:** Indo-Aryan
- **Location:** Sindh, Pakistan and Gujarat, India
- **Speakers:** ~150–200 (classified as endangered)
- **Vitality:** Endangered, with some speakers also fluent in Sindhi.
- **Varieties:** Jikrio Goth Aer and Jamesabad Aer.
- **History:** Influenced by Persian, Arabic, and Turkish during the Delhi Sultanate and Mughal Empire. Spoken in rural Sindh, particularly around Hyderabad and Kunri.

2. Badeshi Language:

- **Family:** Indo-Iranian (unclassified)
- **Location:** Bishigram Valley, Northern Pakistan
- **Speakers:** Critically endangered, with only three speakers found in 2018.
- **Vitality:** At risk of extinction; largely replaced by Torwali.
- **Research:** Efforts by linguists like Zubair Torwali and Muhammad Zaman Sagar to document the language.

3. **Bagri Language:**
   - **Family:** Indo-Aryan
   - **Location:** Northwestern India, Rajasthan, Haryana, Punjab (India)
   - **Speakers:** ~2.34 million (according to the 2011 Census in India)
   - **Vitality:** Developing
   - **Characteristics:** A dialect bridge between Haryanvi, Rajasthani, and Punjabi. Notable for its three lexical tones.
   - **Geographic Distribution:** Found in regions like Bikaner, Sangaria, and Sri Ganganagar in India.

4. **Balochi Language:**
   - **Family:** Indo-European, Western Iranian
   - **Location:** Balochistan (Pakistan, Iran, Afghanistan), Oman, Gulf, and East Africa
   - **Speakers:** 8.8 million (6.28 million in Pakistan)
   - **Vitality:** Vigorous, though literacy is not widespread in Balochi (most speakers are literate in Urdu or Persian).
   - **Dialects:** Includes Southern, Western, and Eastern varieties.
   - **Global Presence:** Spoken in Iran, Afghanistan, and diaspora communities worldwide.

5. **Balti Language:**
   - **Family:** Tibeto-Burman (Tibetic subgroup)
   - **Location:** Gilgit-Baltistan (Pakistan), Ladakh (India)
   - **Speakers:** ~250,000–500,000
   - **Vitality:** Vigorous, with active use among the Balti people in the Baltistan region.
   - **Characteristics:** Shares features with Standard Tibetan, with notable phonological differences.
   - **Dialects:** Four main dialects:

- ♦ **Eastern** (Chorbat and Nubra Valley)
- ♦ **Central** (Khaplu Valley)
- ♦ **Western** (Skardu, Shigar, Rondu)
- ♦ **Southern** (Upper Kharmang, Kargil)

- **Geographic Distribution:** Spoken in regions such as Skardu, Shigar, Kharmang, and Kargil, with some diaspora in cities like Karachi and Lahore.

Language Vitality in Pakistan:

- ♦ **Institutional Languages:** Urdu is the national language, with English as an official language. Other regional languages such as Punjabi, Sindhi, Pashto, and Balochi have a strong presence in their respective areas.
- ♦ **Endangered Languages:** Languages like Aer and Badeshi are critically endangered with very few speakers left.
- ♦ **Developing and Vigorous Languages:** Many languages like Saraiki, Sindhi, Pashto, and Balochi are considered vigorous or developing, with substantial numbers of speakers and active use in cultural, educational, and media contexts.

6. Bateri Language:

- **Language Family:** Indo-Aryan.
- **Location:** Primarily spoken in Kohistan District, Pakistan, and to a lesser extent in Jammu and Kashmir, India.

7. Bhaya Language:

- **Language Family:** Indo-Aryan.
- **Status:** Moribund or possibly extinct.
- **Location:** Spoken in the lower Sindh province, Pakistan.
- **Features:** Belongs to the Western Hindi subgroup, has lexical and morphemic similarities with neighboring languages, and is often misclassified as a dialect.

8. Brahui Language:

- **Language Family:** Dravidian.
- **Location:** Central Balochistan, Pakistan, and parts of Iran, Afghanistan, and Turkmenistan. Small expatriate communities in Iraq, Qatar, and UAE.
- **Features:** Isolated from other Dravidian languages, with theories suggesting either ancient migration or a more recent introduction to Balochistan.
- **Lexicon Composition:**
  - 35% Perso-Arabic origin,
  - 20% Balochi origin,
  - 20% Indo-Aryan origin,
  - 15% Dravidian origin,
  - 10% unknown origin.
- **Genetic Relation:** Brahui speakers are genetically similar to Balochi speakers, not Dravidian speakers.

9. Burushaski Language:

- **Language Family:** Language isolate (no proven relation to other languages).
- **Location:** Spoken by the Burusho people in northern Gilgit-Baltistan, Pakistan, with a few hundred speakers in Jammu and Kashmir, India.
- **Features:** Efforts have been made to link it with various language families, such as North Caucasian, Kartvelian, Yeniseian, or Indo-European, but these are mostly unaccepted.
- **Dialects:**
  - **Hunza and Nagar varieties:** Related but with slight divergence.
  - **Yasin variety:** More divergent, considered by some a distinct language.

- **Influences:** The language has borrowed vocabulary from neighboring languages (e.g., Dardic, Tibeto-Burman, North Caucasian).
- **Jammu & Kashmir Burushaski:** This variety has diverged and shows influences from Kashmiri, Hindi, and Urdu.

10. Chilisso Language:

- **Language Family:** Indo-Aryan.
- **Location:** Spoken by around 1,000 people in eastern Kohistan, Pakistan.

11. Dameli Language:

- **Language Family:** Indo-Aryan (Dardic subgroup).
- **Location:** Spoken by approximately 5,000 people in Domel Town, Chitral District, Khyber-Pakhtunkhwa, Pakistan.
- Features:
    - The language is part of the Dardic subgroup, which is now classified under Indo-Aryan.
    - It has a significant number of words derived from the Nuristani languages.
    - The pronoun system and morphology are characteristic of Dardic languages.
- **Language Contact:** Speakers commonly use Pashto, Khowar, and Urdu, but Dameli remains a vital language in its community.

12. Dari Language:

- **Language Family:** Indo-Iranian (Persian).
- **Location:** Spoken primarily in Afghanistan, particularly in the northern, western, and central regions. Also spoken by Afghan diaspora communities in Iran and Pakistan.
- **Status:**
    - Official language of Afghanistan alongside Pashto.

- Serves as a lingua franca in Afghanistan, with up to 78% of the population speaking it.
- **Historical Context:**
    - Dari is a form of Persian (New Persian), which evolved from Middle Persian (the language of the Sassanian Empire).
    - Historically, it served as the court language during the Sassanid Empire and has deep cultural and historical roots in the region.
- **Mutual Intelligibility:** Dari is mutually intelligible with Iranian Persian, although it has distinct regional vocabulary and pronunciation.
- **Influence on Other Languages:** Dari contributed significantly to vocabulary in South Asian languages such as Urdu, Hindi, Punjabi, and Bengali due to the Persianate influence during the Mughal Empire.

13. Dehwari Language:

- **Language Family**: Southwestern Persian.
- **Location**: Spoken by approximately 19,000 people in Balochistan, Pakistan.
- **Influences**:
    - Dehwari has a significant Brahui influence, making it a Persian dialect with heavy Brahui elements.
    - Many speakers are bilingual in Dehwari and Brahui, with some also fluent in Balochi, Urdu, and English.
- **Cultural Context**: Introduced to Brahui speakers in the 17th century, the language features loanwords from Dehwari in Brahui.

14. Dhatki Language:

- **Language Family**: Indo-Aryan (Rajasthani branch).
- **Location**: Spoken in Tharparkar District, Pakistan, and parts of India (Jaisalmer, Barmer).

- **Speakers**: Ethnically Rajasthanis, Sindhis, and Gujaratis, with a mix of Muslims, Hindus, and traditional folk religions.
- **Dialect Groups**: Western Dhatki (in Pakistan) and Eastern Dhatki (in India).
- **Cultural Context**: Dhatki serves as a unifying language for diverse communities, including Rajputs, Brahmins, and others.

15. Gawar Bati Language:

- **Language Family**: Indo-Aryan (Dardic subgroup).
- **Location**: Spoken by around 9,000 people in Chitral, Pakistan, and across the border in Afghanistan.
- **Features**: Known for its limited study but classified under the Dardic subgroup.
- **Cultural Context**: Gawar-Bati is spoken in the Arandu region, which is the last village in lower Chitral and lies near Afghanistan.

16. Gawri Language:

- **Language Family**: Indo-Aryan (Kohistani subgroup).
- **Location**: Spoken in the Swat Kohistan (Kalam) region and the upper Panjkora River valley in Upper Dir District, Pakistan.
- **Speakers**: Over 200,000 people.
- **Cultural Context**: Often referred to as Kohistani by local speakers, the language is one of several in the northwestern zone of Indo-Aryan languages, closely related to languages like Torwali and Indus Kohistani.

17. Ghera Language:

- **Language Family**: Indo-Aryan (Western Hindi group).
- **Location**: Spoken by around 10,000 people in Hyderabad, Pakistan.
- **Features**: Shares a high percentage of vocabulary with the Gurgula language, but differs significantly in grammar.

18. Goaria Language:

- **Language Family**: Marwari Rajasthani (Indo-Aryan).
- **Location**: Spoken by approximately 25,000 people in Sindh, Pakistan.
- **Cultural Context**: The community is predominantly Hindu, and they use Hindi for worship.

19. Gowro Language:

- **Language Family**: Indo-Aryan.
- **Location**: Spoken in Kohistan District, Pakistan.

20. Gujarati Language:

- **Language Family**: Indo-Aryan (Western zone).
- **Location**: Native to Gujarat, India, and spoken by 55.5 million people.
- **Global Presence**: Gujarati is spoken by diasporas in places such as the United States, the United Kingdom, Kenya, Tanzania, and the UAE.
- **Historical Development**: Evolved from Old Gujarati, which itself descended from Sanskrit, with several stages of linguistic differentiation leading to modern Gujarati.

21. Gujari Language:

- **Region**: Spoken by Gujjars in Jammu & Kashmir, Himachal Pradesh (India), Azad Kashmir, Gilgit-Baltistan (Pakistan), and Afghanistan.
- **Speakers**: Around 1.3 million in India, 400,000 in Pakistan, and 15,000 in Afghanistan.
- **Recognition**: Included in the Sixth Schedule of Jammu and Kashmir's state constitution.
- **Cultural significance**: Rich in folklore, with songs, ballads, and folktales (e.g., "Nooro", "Tajo").
- **Literary tradition**: Poets like Sain Qadar Bakhsh and Javaid Rahi have contributed to creative writing in Gujari.

- **Media**: Broadcasted on All India Radio, Doordarshan, Radio Kashmir, and PTV.
- **Language promotion**: Gujari is taught in schools in Jammu and Kashmir, and universities in India and Pakistan have research centers for it.
- **Revival efforts**: The Gojri Bahali Programme aims to revive Gujari, particularly in Pakistan's urban centers where the language is declining.

22. Gurgula Language:

- **Region**: Spoken by the Gurgula people in Pakistan.
- **Relation**: Similar to the Ghera language but differs significantly in grammar.

23. Hazaragi Dialect:

- **Region**: Spoken by the Hazara people in Afghanistan, Pakistan, Iran, and abroad (e.g., Australia, Europe, USA).
- **Relation**: A variety of Persian, related to Dari, with influences from Turkic and Mongolic languages.
- **Speakers**: Primarily in Hazarajat (Afghanistan), Quetta (Pakistan), and parts of Iran.
- **Recognition**: Hazaragi is being recognized in countries like Australia for immigration and interpreter services.

24. Hindko Language:

- **Region**: Spoken in Khyber Pakhtunkhwa, Punjab (Pakistan), parts of Jammu and Kashmir (India), and by diaspora communities.
- **Speakers**: Estimated 5-7 million speakers.
- **Relation**: A member of the Lahnda dialects, closely related to Punjabi and Saraiki.
- **Cultural influence**: Spoken in areas such as Peshawar, Hazara, and parts of Azad Kashmir.

- **Revitalization**: Some areas are experiencing a shift towards Hindko as a dominant language, displacing other languages like Pashto and Kashmiri.

25. Jadgali Language:

- **Region**: Spoken by the Jadgal people in Pakistan (Balochistan), Iran, and some in Oman.
- **Speakers**: Around 15,600 in Pakistan, 25,000 in Iran.
- **Relation**: A Sindhi dialect closely related to Lasi, underdocumented.
- **Cultural background**: The Jadgali people are of Baloch origin but have adopted a different language due to historical migrations and influences.
- **Current status**: Mostly bilingual with Balochi and Persian being widely spoken.

26. Jandavra Language:

- **Region**: Spoken by the Jandavra people in Sindh, Pakistan, and Jodhpur, India.
- **Family**: Indic language.

27. Jogi Language:

- **Region**: Spoken by the Jogi caste in India and Pakistan, especially in Sindh.
- **Relation**: A dialect of Marwari with distinct pronouns.
- **Speakers**: Hindu and Muslim Jogis.
- **Other Notes**: Some Jogi communities in Sindh speak Sindhi instead of Jogi.

28. Kabutra Language:

- **Region**: Spoken in Sindh, Pakistan.
- **Relation**: Similar to Sansi spoken in India; sometimes written with Arabic script.
- **Status**: Endangered language, with influence from Gujarati.

29. Kalasha Language:

- **Region**: Spoken by the Kalash people in Chitral, Khyber Pakhtunkhwa, Pakistan.
- **Speakers**: Around 4,100.
- **Status**: Endangered, with a language shift to Khowar.
- **Research**: Studies by Gottlieb Wilhelm Leitner, Georg Morgenstierne, Elena Bashir.
- **Features**: Conserves some ancient Dardic features.

30. Kalkoti Language:

- **Region**: Spoken in Kalkot Tehsil, Upper Dir district, Pakistan.
- **Family**: Indo-Aryan.

31. Kamviri Dialect:

- **Region**: Spoken by the Kom people in Afghanistan and Pakistan.
- **Speakers**: 5,000-10,000.
- **Relation**: A dialect of Kamkata-vari.

32. Kashmiri Language:

- **Region**: Spoken by around 7 million people in Jammu and Kashmir (India), and some in Azad Kashmir (Pakistan).
- **Family**: Dardic, Indo-Aryan.
- **Status**: Official language of Jammu and Kashmir (since 2020).
- **Dialects**: Includes Poguli, Kishtwari, and Chenabich Kashir (in the Chenab Valley).
- **Language Shift**: Gradual shift to Urdu and other regional languages.
- **Influence**: Persian (historically), Urdu (currently).

33. Kata-Vari Dialect:

- **Region**: Spoken by the Kata people in Afghanistan and parts of Pakistan (Chitral).

- **Speakers**: Around 40,000 people, mostly in Afghanistan, with around 3,700 in Pakistan.
- **Dialects**: Eastern and Western Kata-vari.
- **Status**: Low literacy rates, less than 1% for native speakers.

34. Khetrani Language:

- Spoken by the Khetran tribe in northeastern Balochistan (Barkhan, Kohlu, and Musakhel Districts).
- Has features similar to Sindhi and Saraiki but is not mutually intelligible with them.
- Historically a dialect continuum of Sindhi and Saraiki, but now limited by the spread of Pashto and Balochi.
- Has few Balochi loanwords and was once considered a remnant of a Dardic language, though this theory is debated.

35. Khowar Language:

- A Dardic language spoken mainly in Chitral and surrounding regions in Pakistan.
- Serves as the lingua franca of Chitral and is related to languages like Standard Punjabi, Sindhi, and Western Pahari.
- Retains many archaic features, with significant Sanskrit influence, and shares morphological similarities with Iranian languages from Badakhshan.

36. Indus Kohistani Language:

- Spoken in the former Kohistan District of Pakistan.
- Often referred to by early researchers as Maiyã (or Mayon), though local use of the term is unverified.

37. Kachi Koli Language:

- A Gujarati subgroup language spoken by the Koli people in India and parts of Sindh, Pakistan.
- Closely related to Parkari Koli and Wadiyara Koli.

38. Parkari Koli Language:

- Spoken in the Tharparkar District of Sindh, Pakistan.
- Part of the broader Koli language group, spoken in the southeastern tip of Sindh, bordering India.

39. Wadiyara Koli Language:

- Spoken by the Wadiyara people, who migrated from Gujarat to Sindh due to famine in the early 20th century.
- Linked to both the Bhil and Koli people but primarily associated with the Koli subgroup.

40. Kundal Shahi Language:

- A highly endangered Indo-Aryan language spoken by a small community in Neelam Valley, Azad Kashmir.
- Speakers are shifting to Hindko, making it vulnerable to extinction.

41. Lasi Dialect:

- A dialect of Sindhi spoken in Balochistan and parts of Sindh, Pakistan.
- Known for borrowing vocabulary from Persian, Balochi, English, and Urdu.

42. Loharki Language:

- A Rajasthani language spoken by a nomadic people in Sindh and Rajasthan.
- Known as "Gade Lohar" in India and "Loharki" in Pakistan.

43. Mankiyali Language:

- A critically endangered Dardic language spoken by a small community in Khyber Pakhtunkhwa, Pakistan.
- It is not mutually intelligible with surrounding languages like Hindko and Gojri but shares some vocabulary with the Kohistani languages.

44. Marwari Language

- **Region**: Predominantly spoken in **Rajasthan**, India, with some speakers in **Gujarat**, **Haryana**, **Eastern Pakistan**, and **Nepal**.
- **Speakers**: Around 7.8 million.
- **Varieties**: Over two dozen varieties, including **Thali**, **Godwari**, **Dhatki**, **Shekhawati**, **Bagri**, and **Merwari**.
- **Script**: Written in **Devanagari** (popular), historically in **Mahajani**, and **Perso-Arabic** in Pakistan (Naskh and Nastalik variants).
- **Mutual Intelligibility**: Closely related to **Gujarati** and **Dingal**, but distinct from both.
- **Cultural Significance**: The language is not officially recognized in India and lacks formal educational status.

45. Mewati Language

- **Region**: Spoken by the **Meo** people in the **Mewat Region** (Rajasthan, Haryana, and parts of Uttar Pradesh).
- **Speakers**: Around 3 million.
- **Linguistic Features**: 9 vowels, 31 consonants, two numbers (singular, plural), two genders (masculine, feminine), and three cases (direct, oblique, vocative).
- **Sentence Structure**: Follows subject–object–verb order, with postpositional case marking and participles functioning as adjectives.
- **Significance**: A defining feature of **Meo** culture.

46. Memoni Language

- **Region**: Spoken by **Kathiawari Memons** in **Kathiawar** (Gujarat), as well as among migrant communities in **Pakistan**, **Sri Lanka**, **South Africa**, and the **US**.
- **Features**: A mixture of **Sindhi**, **Kutchi**, and **Gujarati**. It shares similarities with **Sindhi** and **Kutchi**, but has strong **Gujarati** influences.

- **Script**: Historically written in **Gujarati script**, but **Perso-Arabic** script (Urdu variant) is commonly used.
- **Cultural Context**: Exclusively spoken by **Muslim Memons** of Kathiawar origin, distinguishing them from other Memon sub-groups.

47. Od Language

- **Region**: Spoken by the **Od** people in parts of **Gujarat**, **Rajasthan**, **Haryana**, **New Delhi**, **Punjab**, and **Sindh**.
- **Speakers**: Around 2 million.
- **Linguistic Features**: Similar to **Marathi**, with influences from **Gujarati** and **Punjabi**.
- **Preservation Efforts**: Communities like **Oadki Rakarhanga** are working towards preserving the language.

48. Ormuri Language

- **Region**: Spoken by the **Burki** people in **South Waziristan** (Pakistan) and parts of **Logar Province**, **Afghanistan**.
- **Speakers**: Very few, considered endangered.
- **Linguistic Features**: Part of the **Eastern Iranian** group, with unique phonetic features like voiceless alveolar trill.
- **Cultural Context**: Historically significant, with mentions by **Babar** in his autobiography and a rich tribal history.

49. Pahari-Pothwari Language

- **Region**: Spoken in **Pothohar Plateau** (northern Punjab, Pakistan), **Azad Kashmir**, and **Jammu & Kashmir** (India).
- **Varieties**: Includes **Pothwari**, **Mirpuri**, and **Pahari** dialects. Pothwari is the most prestigious.
- **Mutual Intelligibility**: Transitionary between **Hindko** and **Punjabi**, with significant overlap with **Standard Punjabi**.
- **Script**: Written in **Shahmukhi** script.
- **Significance**: Important for the local culture, and with a notable diaspora, especially in the **UK** due to migration from **Mirpur**.

50. Pahari Language:

- Spoken in parts of Indian Jammu and Kashmir, particularly in Poonch and Rajouri districts, as well as areas like Baramulla and Kupwara.
- It is sometimes conflated with Western Pahari languages (like Bhadarwahi), but they are distinct but related.
- It is listed as a regional language in the Constitution of Jammu and Kashmir.

51. Indo-Pakistani Sign Language (IPSL):

- Used by approximately 15 million deaf signers in South Asia.
- It is the most used sign language globally and ranks as the 151st most "spoken" language according to Ethnologue (2021).

52. Palula Language:

- Spoken by about 10,000 people in the valleys of Ashret and Biori in Chitral District, Pakistan.
- A Dardic language with significant shifting to Khowar in some villages.
- Well-documented by several linguists including George Morgenstierne and Kendall Decker.

53. Pashto Varieties:

- **Central Pashto**: Standard variety spoken in parts of Pakistan and Afghanistan; affected by the "Great Karlāṇ Vowel Shift."
- **Northern Pashto**: Spoken in Khyber Pakhtunkhwa, Pakistan, including the Northwestern and Northeastern dialects.
- **Southern Pashto**: Known as Kandahārí Pashto, spoken in southern Afghanistan; preserves archaic phonological features.

54. Punjabi Language:

- An Indo-Aryan language spoken in the Punjab region (both Pakistan and India) and by a large diaspora worldwide.
- Approximately 113 million native speakers.
- Written in Shahmukhi (Perso-Arabic) script in Pakistan and Gurmukhi in India.
- Known for its lexical tone, developed from Prakrit and Apabhraṃśa, with influences from Arabic, Persian, and Urdu.

55. Saraiki Language:

- Spoken by 26 million people in southwestern Punjab, Pakistan.
- Related to Punjabi but distinct due to differences in phonology, grammar, and influences from Sindhi.
- Became a distinct language identity in the 1960s.
- Classified as part of the Western Punjabi subgroup of Indo-Aryan languages.

56. Sarikoli Language:

Language Classification:

- ♦ Sarikoli, also known as Sariqoli, Selekur, Sarikul, Sariqul, or Sariköli, belongs to the Pamir subgroup of Southeastern Iranian languages.
- ♦ It is spoken by the Pamiris of Xinjiang, China.

Official Status:

- ♦ In China, Sarikoli is officially referred to as the "Tajik language."
- ♦ It differs from Tajik, the Iranian language spoken in Tajikistan, which is a dialect of Persian.

Linguistic Distinctions:

- ♦ Sarikoli is an Eastern Iranian language related to other Pamir languages in Tajikistan and Afghanistan.

- Western Iranian languages like Farsi-Dari-Tajik are distinctly different and geographically separated from Sarikoli.

Historical and Alternative Names:

- Sarikoli is also called Tashkorghani, named after the ancient Sarikoli kingdom's capital (now Tashkurgan in Xinjiang, China).
- Scholars predominantly use "Sarikoli," though variations like "Selekuri" appear due to Chinese phonetic transcriptions.

Speaker Population and Distribution:

- There are approximately 35,000 speakers, primarily in the Taxkorgan Tajik Autonomous County, Xinjiang, China.
- A smaller number of speakers reside in the Pakistani-administered region of Kashmir, near the China-Pakistan border.

Language Interaction:

- Sarikoli speakers often use Chinese and Uyghur for communication with other ethnic groups in the region.

57. Sawi Language:

- **Classification**: Endangered Indo-Aryan language in the Shina language cluster, Dardic subgroup.
- **Geography**: Spoken in Sau village, Kunar River, Afghanistan, and near Chitral in Pakistan.
- **Speakers**: Associated with the Gawar ethnic group; they use Pashto to communicate with neighboring groups.
- **History**: Many displaced to refugee camps during unrest but have largely returned.
- **Relations**: Closely related to Southern Palula in Ashret (Chitral), indicating a shared migration history from Diamer District.

58. Shina Language:

- **Classification**: Dardic language of the Indo-Aryan family.
- **Geography**: Predominantly spoken in Gilgit-Baltistan, Kohistan, parts of Azad Kashmir, and Ladakh (India).
- **Population**: Around 1.15 million in Pakistan and 32,200 in India (2011 census).
- **Characteristics**: Primarily spoken; limited written tradition with multiple writing systems proposed.
- **Influence**: Borrowed heavily from Urdu, Punjabi, Arabic, and Persian.
- **Outliers**: Includes varieties like Palula, Sawi, Brokskat, Ushojo, and Kalkoti.

59. Kohistani Shina Language:

- **Classification**: Indo-Aryan language spoken in Kohistan, Pakistan.
- **Characteristics**: Mutually intelligible with Shina of Chilas but not the Gilgit standard dialect.
- **Speakers**: Bateri and Kalkoti speakers often use it as a second language.
- **Documentation**: Grammar and dictionaries are available.

60. Sindhi Language:

- **Classification**: Indo-Aryan language with over 30 million speakers in Sindh, Pakistan, and 1.7 million in India.
- **Scripts**: Primarily uses Perso-Arabic in Pakistan and Perso-Arabic/Devanagari in India.
- **History**: Influenced by Arabic and Persian since the 8th century. Modern development under British rule (1843).
- **Literature**: Rich tradition, including Sufi poetry and romantic folktales. Shah Abdul Latif Bhittai is a renowned poet.
- **Modern Usage**: Diverging styles in Pakistan (influenced by Urdu) and India (influenced by Hindi).

61. Sindhi Bhil Language:

- **Classification**: Indo-Aryan dialect of Sindhi spoken by the Bhil people in Sindh and Balochistan, Pakistan.
- **Characteristics**: Retains many old Sindhi words lost in modern Sindhi due to Arabic, Persian, and Chaghatai influences.
- **Dialects**: Includes Badin (close to Sindhi) and Mohrano (influenced by Dhatki).
- **Speakers**: 86,500 primarily Hindu Sindhi Bhils and Meghwars, with some diasporas in India (Gujarat and Delhi).

62. Tamil Language:

The Tamil language, a member of the Dravidian language family, is one of the most significant and ancient languages of South Asia and the world. Its rich history, vast literature, and extensive geographic distribution make it a cornerstone of cultural identity for Tamil-speaking communities globally. Below is a structured summary of key aspects of the Tamil language:

Historical and Cultural Significance

- **Antiquity**: Tamil is among the world's oldest surviving classical languages, with a documented history spanning over 2,000 years.
- **Classical Recognition**: It was the first language to be declared a "classical language" of India, recognized for its antiquity and literary richness.
- **Earliest Literature**: Sangam literature (c. 300 BCE–300 CE) is one of the oldest literary traditions, reflecting Tamil society's early values and culture.
- **Epigraphic Evidence**: Tamil-Brahmi inscriptions date back to the 3rd century BCE, found in India, Sri Lanka, Thailand, and Egypt, highlighting its ancient trade and cultural connections.

- **Global Influence**: Tamil inscriptions, artifacts, and linguistic loans indicate early Tamil influence on languages like Biblical Hebrew and evidence of its role as a maritime trade lingua franca.

Linguistic Characteristics:

- **Family**: Belongs to the Dravidian language family and shares a close relationship with Malayalam.
- **Evolution**: Classified into three stages:
  - Old Tamil (300 BCE–700 CE): Ancient inscriptions and Sangam literature.
  - Middle Tamil (700–1600 CE): Evolution of phonology and grammar.
  - Modern Tamil (1600 CE–present): Influence of European languages and linguistic purism.
- **Literary Standards**: Modern written Tamil adheres to Middle Tamil grammar as codified in the *Nannūl*.
- **Phonological Changes**: Notable shifts include vowel modifications and the disappearance of the aytam phoneme.

Global Presence:

- **India**: Official language of Tamil Nadu and Puducherry; spoken in parts of Kerala, Karnataka, Andhra Pradesh, and Telangana.
- **Sri Lanka**: An official language and the mother tongue of Tamils and some Sri Lankan Moors.
- **Singapore**: One of the official languages.
- **Diaspora**: Significant communities in Malaysia, South Africa, Canada, Australia, Europe, and the Middle East. Tamil-speaking migrants and their descendants also exist in the Americas, Réunion, and Mauritius.

Cultural and Religious Role:

- **Tamil Sangams**: Historical assemblies organized for the development of Tamil literature.

- **Sacred Connection**: Revered as a divine language in Hindu traditions; associated with Lord Shiva and the Tamil God, Murugan.
- **Modern Literary Movements**: The Pure Tamil Movement aimed to remove Sanskrit influences and promote linguistic purism.

Writing and Publishing:

- **Scripts**: Historically written in Tamil-Brahmi; now uses the modern Tamil script.
- **First Printed Indian Language**: *Thambiran Vanakkam* (1578) was the first Tamil book printed.
- **Newspapers**: A robust print culture, with thousands of publications in Tamil.

Contemporary Issues and Contributions:

- **Language Policy**: Advocated as a medium of education and public administration in Tamil Nadu and Sri Lanka.
- **Cultural Revival**: Tamil communities in countries like Réunion have revived interest in the language.
- **Technology and Media**: Tamil is extensively used in digital media, education, and entertainment globally.

Tamil's historical roots and global reach continue to make it a vibrant and influential language, celebrated for its continuity and cultural depth.

1. **Torwali Language**: An Indo-Aryan language spoken by the Torwali people in Bahrain and Chail areas of Swat District, Pakistan.
    - **Origins**: Developed from pre-Muslim communities of Swat, closely related to Niya, a dialect of Gāndhārī.
    - **Endangered Status**: Classified as "definitely endangered" by UNESCO and "vulnerable" by the Catalogue of Endangered Languages.

- **Revitalization Efforts**: Language revitalization began in 2004, with community-based mother-tongue schools established by Idara Baraye Taleem-o-Taraqi (IBT).

2. **Urdu Language:** Indo-Aryan language primarily spoken in South Asia, official in Pakistan and several states in India; also spoken in Nepal, South Africa, Afghanistan, and Bangladesh.
   - **Historical Background:** Evolved from Hindustani, with a mix of Sanskrit, Prakrit, and Persian influences; Urdu and Hindi are mutually intelligible in colloquial speech.
   - **Colonial Period:** Became an official language of British India in 1837, replacing Persian. The British promoted Urdu in Muslim-majority regions to counter Persian influence.
   - **Linguistic Development:** Urdu emerged as a literary language in the 18th century, with standard forms developing in Delhi, Lucknow, and Karachi. It adopted the Persian script (Nastaleeq).
   - **Naming:** The term "Urdu" was first used by poet Ghulam Hamadani Mushafi in 1780, deriving from the Turkic word "Ordu" (army) as "language of the camp."
   - **Colonial Impact:** British referred to the language as "Moors" or "Moorish jargon." The British standardization and teaching of Urdu in schools cemented its association with Muslims in colonial India.
   - **Post-Independence:** In Pakistan, Urdu was chosen as the national language to unify diverse linguistic groups. Despite competition from regional languages, Urdu remains central to Pakistani identity.
   - **Sociopolitical Factors:** The language became a tool for Muslim identity in India, while in Pakistan, it struggled against regional languages and English.
   - **Decline and Debate:** Urdu's prominence has declined in India, with fewer Hindus using it and Muslims switching to Hindi due to socio-economic factors. There

is debate about its preservation through the Perso-Arabic script or transliteration into Devanagari or Roman script.

- **Cultural Influence:** Despite challenges, Urdu remains influential in Indian pop culture, particularly Bollywood. In Pakistan, it has been associated with religious Islamism and political conservatism.
- **Modern Challenges:** The language faces challenges of fading knowledge of its script and a decline in its use in education and official settings, while English increasingly dominates.

Demographic and Geographic Distribution:

- **Native Speakers**: Over 100 million Urdu speakers in India and Pakistan combined:
  - India: 50.8 million (4.34% of the population as per 2011 census)
  - Pakistan: 16 million (2006 data)
- **Other Countries**: Significant Urdu-speaking populations in the UK, Saudi Arabia, the US, and Bangladesh.
- **Hindustani**: Urdu is a variety of Hindustani, which is the third most spoken language globally (after Mandarin and English).
- **Dialects**: Urdu in Pakistan is influenced by regional languages, creating a distinct Pakistani variant. In India, regional dialects like Standard Urdu (Lucknow, Delhi) and Dakhni (South India) exist.
- **Pakistan**: Urdu is widely spoken and understood, though it is the native language of only 7% of the population. It serves as a unifying language for the country, with millions of non-native speakers learning it.
- **India**: Urdu is spoken in regions with large Muslim populations (e.g., Uttar Pradesh, Telangana, Maharashtra, Bihar). Indian cities like Hyderabad, Lucknow, Delhi, and Bangalore are major centers of Urdu.

- **Elsewhere**: It's spoken by South Asian migrants in urban centers in the Gulf, UK, US, Canada, Germany, and Australia.

Cultural Identity:

- **Colonial India**: Urdu developed as a marker of Islamic identity in British India, in contrast to Hindi which was associated with Hindu identity.
- **Pakistan**: Urdu became a symbol of unity in post-1947 Pakistan, though regional tensions over language, especially with Bengali in East Pakistan (now Bangladesh), challenged its role.
- **Religious Influence**: Urdu adopted the Persian-Arabic script due to its connection to Islam, and this association with Islam continues to shape its cultural identity.

Official Status:

- **Pakistan**: Urdu is the national and one of the official languages, though English is used in higher government echelons. Urdu is widely used for education, literature, and business, despite being the mother tongue of only a small percentage of Pakistanis.
- **India**: Urdu is an official language in several Indian states (e.g., Uttar Pradesh, Bihar, Telangana) and has a significant presence in literature, media, and religious schools (Madrasa).
    - The promotion of Urdu in India faces challenges, especially with the stronger promotion of Hindi.

Comparison with Hindi:

- **Mutual Intelligibility**: Urdu and Hindi are considered two standard registers of the same language (Hindustani), sharing a core vocabulary and grammar. Differences lie mainly in script and vocabulary:
    - **Urdu** uses the Nastaliq Persian script and incorporates Persian and Arabic loanwords.
    - **Hindi** uses Devanagari script and has more Sanskrit-derived vocabulary.

- **Sociolinguistic Differences**: The languages are often seen as distinct due to political and religious factors, especially after the Partition of India in 1947.

3. **Ushoji:** An Indo-Aryan language spoken in Kohistan and Swat districts of Pakistan, closely related to other regional languages.
4. **Vaghri:** Spoken in parts of Pakistan, Vaghri is an Indo-Aryan language with variants like Wagdi and Bauria, but it's unclear whether these are distinct languages or dialects.
5. **Wakhi:** A part of the Eastern Iranian branch of Indo-European languages, spoken by a small population in Pakistan, Afghanistan, Tajikistan, and China, particularly in the Wakhan Corridor and Gilgit-Baltistan. Despite being overshadowed by more dominant languages like Urdu and English, efforts are being made to preserve and promote the language and its cultural heritage.
6. **Wanetsi:** A dialect of Pashto spoken by the Spin Tareen tribe in Balochistan, Pakistan, and parts of Afghanistan. This language is considered by some linguists to be an archaic or early form of Pashto, with unique linguistic features that distinguish it from other Pashto dialects.
7. **Yidgha:** An Eastern Iranian language, closely related to Munji, spoken in the upper Lotkoh Valley in Chitral. This language, along with others in Chitral, reflects the region's incredible linguistic diversity.

These languages serve as important markers of identity and culture for their respective communities. Many of them are endangered, with only a few thousand speakers left, and face pressure from dominant languages like Urdu and English. Linguists continue to study these languages, which often serve as critical sources of cultural knowledge, historical ties, and regional connections for the people who speak them. Efforts such as the Wakhi Cultural Association's work in Pakistan highlight the ongoing efforts to preserve these languages through music, literature, and community programs.

Official Languages of Pakistan

Urdu (Official Language):

- National language and lingua franca of Pakistan.
- Spoken as a second language by the majority of Pakistanis (only 7% speak it as a first language).
- Chosen in 1947 for national unity among diverse linguistic communities.
- Used in education, media, and government across all provinces.
- Absorbs vocabulary from regional languages, contributing to its rich linguistic diversity.
- Taught as a compulsory subject in schools up to higher secondary level.

English (Co-official Language):

- Co-official language alongside Urdu.
- Widely used in government, legal systems, and education (especially higher education).

- The language of official business, particularly in the executive, legislative, and judicial branches.
- Seen as a language of upward mobility and prestige, commonly spoken in urban and elite circles.
- Increasingly prominent in schools, colleges, and universities as a medium of instruction.
- Efforts to promote Urdu in official business while maintaining English's role in education and government.

Both languages are integral to communication, culture, and access to opportunities in Pakistan.

Major Regional Languages of Pakistan

Punjabi:

- Indo-Aryan language, most widely spoken in Pakistan (38.78% of Pakistanis).
- Primary dialect: Majha, written in **Shahmukhi script**.
- Also spoken by significant **overseas diaspora** (Canada, UK, USA).
- Known for **lexical tone**, which is unusual in Indo-Aryan languages.

Pashto:

- Iranian language spoken by 18.24% of Pakistanis, mainly in **Khyber Pakhtunkhwa** and northern **Balochistan**.
- Significant Pashtun population in major cities like **Karachi**, **Islamabad**, and **Rawalpindi**.
- Three major dialects: **Northern**, **Southern**, and **Wanetsi**.

Sindhi:

- Indo-Aryan language spoken by around 15% of Pakistanis, mainly in the **Sindh** province.
- Derived from **Sanskrit** and **Prakrit** roots, evolving in stages since the 10th century CE.
- Six major dialects: **Siroli**, **Vicholi**, **Lari**, **Thari**, **Lasi**, and **Kutchi**.

Saraiki:

- Indo-Aryan language of the **Lahnda** group, spoken in **southern Punjab** and parts of **Khyber Pakhtunkhwa**, **Sindh**, and **Balochistan**.
- Mutually intelligible with **Punjabi** but differs in phonology, lacking tones, and with influences from **Sindhi**.
- Spoken by approximately **26 million** people.

Balochi:

- Iranian language spoken by about **3%** of Pakistanis, primarily in **Balochistan**.
- Major dialect: **Rakshani** with sub-dialects like **Kalati**, **Chagai-Kharani**, and **Panjguri**.
- **Eastern Hill Balochi** (Northern) is distinct from other dialects.

Hindko:

- Cover term for various **Lahnda** dialects spoken in **northwestern Pakistan** (Khyber Pakhtunkhwa and parts of Punjab).
- Mutually intelligible with **Punjabi** and **Saraiki**, with more affinities to **Saraiki**.
- Often called **Hindki** locally.

Brahui:

- **Dravidian language** spoken by a minority in **central Balochistan** (Kalat, Khuzdar, Mastung).

- A minority language with declining speakers due to influence from other regional languages.

These languages reflect the **linguistic diversity** of Pakistan, with each having its unique geographical, cultural, and historical significance.

Endengered languages of Pakistan:

Balti:

- Tibetic language spoken by the **Balti people** in **Baltistan** (Gilgit-Baltistan, Pakistan), **Nubra Valley** (India), and **Kargil**.
- Retains many Old Tibetan sounds, unlike Standard Tibetan.
- Uses a **simple pitch accent system** (unlike the complex pitch system of Standard Tibetan).
- Expanding its vocabulary due to influences from **Urdu**, **Punjabi**, **English**, **Arabic**, and **Persian**.

Gawri Language:

- Also known as **Kalami** or **Bashkarik**, spoken in **Swat Kohistan** (Kalam) and the **upper Swat** and **Panjkora river valley** regions of **Khyber Pakhtunkhwa**, Pakistan.

Badeshi Language:

- Unclassified **Indo-Iranian language**, critically endangered, spoken in northern Pakistan.
- Very few speakers remain, with only around **three speakers** found in 2018.
- Efforts by linguists like **Muhammad Zaman Sagar** and **Zubair Torwali** are ongoing to document it.

Bateri Language:

- **Indo-Aryan language** spoken mainly in **Kohistan District**, Pakistan, and to a lesser extent in **Jammu and Kashmir**, India.

Bhadarwahi:

- **Indo-Aryan language** spoken in the **Bhadarwah** region of **Jammu and Kashmir**, India.
- Includes related dialects: **Bhalesi** and **Khasali**.
- **Bhadarwahi** is a lingua franca in the region.

Bruhui Language:

- **Dravidian language** spoken by the **Brahui people** in central **Balochistan** (Pakistan), and also in **Iran**, **Afghanistan**, and **Turkmenistan**.
- Isolated from Dravidian speakers in **South India**, but retains distinct features.
- Spoken in districts like **Kalat**, **Khuzdar**, **Mastung**, and **Quetta**.

Burushaski:

- **Language isolate** spoken by the **Burusho people** in **northern Gilgit-Baltistan** (Hunza, Nagar, Yasin, and Ghizer valleys), Pakistan.
- Some speakers in **Jammu and Kashmir**, India, where it has been influenced by **Kashmiri**, **Hindi**, and **Urdu**.
- Yasin variety is distinct, with **low intelligibility** with other dialects.
- Around **120,000** speakers in Pakistan and a few hundred in India.

Chilisso Language:

- **Indo-Aryan language** spoken by about **1,000 people** in **eastern Kohistan**, Pakistan.

Dameli Language:

- **Indo-Aryan language** spoken by about **5,000 people** in the **Domel Town** of **Chitral District**, Khyber Pakhtunkhwa, Pakistan.

- **Pashto, Khowar**, and **Urdu** are spoken as second languages, but Dameli remains in use in local villages.

Dawoodi Language:

- **Endangered Indo-Aryan language** spoken by a few hundred people in **Gilgit-Baltistan**.
- Historically related to **Central Indo-Aryan** languages, influenced by neighboring languages like **Shina** and **Burushaski**.
- Speakers are proficient in other local languages and **Urdu**.

Gawar-Bati Language:

- An Indo-Aryan language spoken in Chitral, Pakistan, and across the border in Afghanistan. It has around 9,000 speakers and is classified as a Dardic language.

Gowro Language:

- Spoken in Kohistan District, Pakistan, it belongs to the Indo-Aryan family.

Jadgali Language:

- A dialect of Sindhi spoken by the Jadgal ethnic group in Pakistan and Iran, with communities in Oman. It is critically underdocumented and holds historical significance in the linguistic study of Balochistan and Brahui.

Kalasha Language:

- Spoken by the Kalash people in the Chitral District, Pakistan, with about 4,100 speakers. It is endangered and shifting towards Khowar. Kalasha retains several archaic features of the Dardic languages.

Kalkoti Language:

- Spoken in the Kalkot Tehsil, Upper Dir District, Pakistan, it is another Indo-Aryan language of the region.

Kamkata-Vari Language:

- A large Nuristani language spoken by 40,000 to 60,000 people in both Afghanistan and Pakistan. It includes dialects such as Kamviri and Kata-Vari.

Khowar:

- The lingua franca of Chitral, Pakistan, spoken by about 300,000 people. Khowar shares many features with other Indo-Aryan languages and has influenced the local culture and other languages in the region.

Kundal Shahi Language:

- Spoken in Neelam Valley, Azad Kashmir, by around 700 people, it is endangered and shifting towards Hindko.

Indus Kohistani Language:

- Spoken in the Kohistan region of Pakistan, it is an Indo-Aryan language related to other languages of the region.

Ormuri:

- An endangered Eastern Iranian language spoken in parts of Afghanistan and Waziristan, Pakistan, by the Ormur tribe. It has a unique sound system and is threatened by language shift towards Pashto and Dari.

Ormuri Tribe (Baraki):

- The Ormuri tribe is also known as Baraki.
- Historically, there were 8,000-10,000 Ormuri families in the Logar area in the early 19th century and 400-500 families in Kaniguram by the early 20th century.
- The tribe lives in mixed communities with Tajiks and Pashtuns in Afghanistan, and mainly with Pashtuns in Pakistan.
- Historical Origins:

- Traced back to Herodotus, mentioning the Persian Emperor Darius Hystaspes and the settlement of the Baraki people in Bactria.
- The village of Barke, where they lived, was still inhabited in 1891.
- Language:
- The name "Ormuri" is derived from Pashto, meaning "fire."
- The Ormuri language was first mentioned by Babur, the founder of the Mughal Empire, in his memoirs, Baburnama.
- Many Ormuri speakers are bilingual, speaking Pashto, Persian, Dari, or Kaboli.
- Cultural Influence:
- Pir Roshan, a key figure in Pashto literature, incorporated Ormuri words into his book Khairul-Bayan.
- Linguistic Classification:
- Ormuri is part of the Eastern Iranian group of languages.
- The language has influences from Pashto, Persian, and Greek due to historical interactions.
- Current Status:
- The Ormuri language, like many other regional languages, is at risk but remains vital in some communities.
- Efforts to preserve and revitalize endangered languages like Torwali, Palula, and Wakhi are ongoing.
- Broader Linguistic Diversity:
- Other regional languages include Palula, Purgi, Sawi, Wakhi, Yidgha, Torwali, and Zangskari.
- Many of these languages face endangerment but are still spoken in certain regions.

Palula Language:

- An Indo-Aryan language spoken by around 10,000 people in the valleys of Ashret and Biori, and some villages like Puri and Kalkatak in Chitral District, Pakistan.

- Classified as a Dardic language, Palula is vibrant in some areas, although some villages are shifting to Khowar.
- The language faces endangerment, though it remains strong in the main settlements.

Purgi Language:

- A Tibetic language related to Balti, spoken by the Purigpa people in Ladakh, India, and Baltistan, Pakistan.
- Most speakers are Shia Muslims, with some Buddhists and Noorbakhshi/Sunni Muslims.
- Closely related to Balti, though its status as a separate language or a variety of Balti is debated.

Sawi Language:

- An endangered Indo-Aryan language spoken in northeastern Afghanistan and northwestern Pakistan.
- Classified within the Shina language group, spoken in the village of Sau, near the Kunar River.
- Shares a linguistic relationship with Palula, with some speakers considering the two as related.

Spiti Bhoti:

- A Tibetic language spoken in the Spiti Valley, India.
- Part of the Lahauli-Spiti language group.

Torwali Language:

- An endangered Indo-Aryan language spoken in Swat, Pakistan.
- Closely related to Niya, an ancient Gandhari dialect, and classified as "vulnerable" by UNESCO.
- Efforts are being made to revitalize the language, with community schools and support from organizations like Idara Baraye Taleem-o-Taraqi.

Ushoji Language:

- An Indo-Aryan language spoken in Kohistan and Swat districts, Pakistan.

Wakhi Language:

- An Eastern Iranian language spoken in Afghanistan, Tajikistan, northern Pakistan, and western China.
- Part of the Pamir language group, with a significant population in Pakistan's Gilgit-Baltistan region.
- Wakhi is used by a community known as the Pamiris and faces language revitalization efforts, including cultural programs by the Wakhi Cultural Association in Pakistan.

Yidgha Language:

- An Eastern Iranian language spoken in the upper Lotkoh Valley, Chitral, Pakistan.
- Similar to the Munji language spoken in Afghanistan.

Zangskari Language:

- An endangered Tibetic language spoken in the Zanskar region of Ladakh, India.
- Divided into four dialects, each spoken in different regions of Zanskar.

Other Regional Languages of Pakistan:

- Includes Balochi, Balti, Brahui, Burushaski, Dhatki, Gujari, Hazaragi, Hinko, Kashmiri, Khowar, Kohistani, Kyrgyz, Marwari, Pashto, Punjabi, Pahari-Pothwari, Parkari Koli, Saraiki, Shina, Sindhi, Turkmen, Uzbek, and Pakistani Sign Language.